THE DIARY OF AN
ARTILLERY
OFFICER
The 1st Canadian Divisional Artillery
on the Western Front

GOC RA Canadian Corps and some of his staff near Passchendaele, late October/ early November, 1917. Rear row from left: Captain Lennox P. Napier; Captain Lewis G. McNab; and Captain Orland H. Linton, Staff Captain Canadian Corps Heavy Artillery. Front row from left: unidentified Captain; Lieutenant Colonel Andrew G. L. McNaughton, CBSO Canadian Corps; Brigadier General Edward W. B. Morrison, DSO, GOC RA Canadian Corps; Major Alan F. Brooke, Staff Officer GOC RA Canadian Corps; and Major Richard J. Leach, MC, Brigade Major Canadian Corps Heavy Artillery. (*Courtesy of the RCA Museum*)

THE DIARY OF AN
ARTILLERY OFFICER

The 1st Canadian Divisional Artillery on the Western Front

MAJOR ARTHUR HARDIE BICK DSO
EDITED BY PETER HARDIE BICK

AMBERLEY

Emblem of the Canadian Artillery: 'Everywhere, Where Right and Glory Lead'.

First published 2011

Amberley Publishing
Cirencester Road, Chalford,
Stroud, Gloucestershire, GL6 8PE

www.amberleybooks.com

British Library Cataloguing in Publication Data.
A catalogue record for this book is available from the British Library.

ISBN 978-1-4456-0270-7

Typeset in 10.5pt on 13pt Sabon.
Typesetting and Origination by Amberley Publishing.
Printed in the UK.

Contents

Detail taken from picture on p. 135. (*Courtesy of the RCA Museum*)

Maps

WAR DIARY
or
INTELLIGENCE SUMMARY.

(Erase heading not required.)

Instructions regarding War Diaries and Intelligence Summaries are contained in F.S. Regs., Part II. and the Staff Manual respectively. Title pages will be prepared in manuscript.

Place	Date	Hour	Summary of Events and Information	Remarks and references to Appendices
BERLES	20.			
BERLES	21			
BERLES	22.			

A page from the handwritten diary.

Acknowledgements

This document uses as its main source the handwritten war diaries that Major A. H. Bick DSO wrote daily as Brigade Major of the 1st Canadian Divisional Artillery from December 1917 to February 1919, covering artillery related events of the final battles of the First World War. These documents and other information were initially made available to me on microfilm by the Library and Archives of Canada. They have been digitised since then and placed on the internet by the LAC.

First and foremost I would like to thank Lieutenant Colonel Brian Reid, a member of the Royal Regiment of Canadian Artillery, who has carefully reviewed more than one draft of the text and has offered many useful suggestions on aspects of artillery practices in the First World War. He has also offered much encouragement throughout the project.

I am indebted to my sisters, Daphne Robertson McCleod and Iris Beare, for drawing my attention to the fact that the Library and Archives of Canada contained so much information relating to Major Bick's military career in the First World War.

The contemporary account of the battles of 1918, written by Lieutenant General A. W. Currie in 1919, has provided the background to these dramatic events. The maps he used to illustrate them have been used again, with some added information, to give substance to the commentaries that I have written.

For the material used in my commentaries, I have been greatly assisted by both the Imperial War Museum Library and the British Library in London. These libraries have given me access to a wide range of literature about the First World War. Mr Marc George, the curator of the Canadian Artillery Museum, Shilo, has provided almost all of the excellent photographic illustrations. Mr J. K. White of Toronto has kept me up to date with the most recently published material; Mr Alexander Townson of Ottawa searched for and found the photograph, in the LAC, of the staff group of the 1st Canadian Divisional Artillery; Mr Elliott Parker of Brockville has provided vital links with the Grierson family; Mr Paul Banfield of Queen's University, Kingston, where Arthur Hardie Bick studied engineering from 1909 to 1914, has provided information about his time there; Mrs Doris Grierson Hope of Ottawa has assisted me in contacting Canadian Government Departments, especially the Directorate of History and Heritage (DHH) in the Department of National Defense; the Chief Archivist of DHH, Mr Warren Sinclair, has given me both advice and valuable introductions to members of the military establishment; Dr W. Van der Kloot has given me valuable advice on the use of sound ranging in the First World War; the Canadian Expeditionary Force Study Group has provided explanations of some of the more obscure abbreviations used; the Curator of the Royal Artillery Museum, Mr Paul Evans, has offered advice on some of the illustrations and sources of information about German artillery; Mrs Avril Willshaw of Rottingdean edited early versions of the manuscript; and Dr Gerald Mars suggested the format of an edited version of the diaries with added commentaries.

I could not have completed the work on this document without the help and encouragement of my wife Jill over the years of research and lengthy correspondence with the many sources that have provided vital information, enabling me to write knowledgeably about the First World War.

Peter Hardie Bick
Rottingdean
November 2010

Foreword

My grandfather fought in the 3rd Canadian Infantry Battalion of the 1st Canadian Infantry Division in the First World War. Somehow, against all the odds, he made it through from November 1916 to the Armistice and beyond to return home to Fort Erie, Ontario, in 1919. It is not going out too far on a limb to note that the policy of Lieutenant General Sir Arthur Currie, the commander of the magnificent Canadian Expeditionary Force (CEF), to pound the Germans with every artillery round available, played no little part in my grandfather's survival. Furthermore, he knew that, even in those relatively technically unsophisticated times, there was more to employing artillery than merely lining up the guns, piling mountains of ammunition behind them, and shouting 'Go to 'er, boys!'

The CEF indeed had a reputation as the 'shock troops' of the British Empire. In the period covered by this book, the Canadians broke through the German lines at Amiens and fought their way across France and Belgium. There was a certain amount of delicious irony in that on 11 November 1918 Canadian infantrymen liberated the Belgian city of Mons, where British soldiers first met Germans in battle in 1914. In doing so, the CEF suffered heavy casualties, but shattered every German division it encountered in a series of brilliantly planned and executed battles. This last three months of the war entered Canadian lore as 'Canada's Hundred Days'.

As hinted above, no little part of the Canadian reputation was because of their superb artillery, which was both innovative, boldly handled and responsive to the needs of the infantry it supported. This was especially true of the guns and trench mortars of the 1st Canadian Division, and this is where the author of the war diaries that form the basis of this book comes into play. Major Arthur Hardie Bick was already a veteran when he was posted to the Headquarters, Royal Artillery of the 1st Division as the Brigade Major, or the principal artillery staff officer in the division. In the pages he penned daily we can identify a precise, calculating mind, with the ability to zero in on the main issues of the day, and solve them. My grandfather and his comrades were well served by the major and his brothers-in-arms.

There are a few surprises in this book. Rather than give them away, I will just mention one. The High Command of the British Armies in France were, in popular lore, donkeys leading lions. Maybe so, but in the 'backs to the wall' time of peril in the German Spring offensive of 1918, we find that Field Marshall Haig had the foresight to keep the CEF out of the fray. Moreover, the Canadians began to train in offensive tactics and mobile operations for the great counterstroke that led to victory in 1918.

I came to this book by a roundabout manner. Earlier this year I was approached by Dr Steve Harris of the Canadian Department of National Defense's Director of History and Heritage and Brigadier General (retired) Ernest B. Beno, the Colonel Commandant of the Royal Regiment of Canadian Artillery, to see if I was willing to read and help edit a book based on some First World War diaries. The task has been a real pleasure. Not only did I learn quite a lot about the practice of the gunners' art of a century past, but I found much to link their mastery of the craft with today's Canadian artillerymen. You see, I am also preparing the history of my regiment's part in the present war in Afghanistan. I suspect Arthur Bick would readily take to the computers and the lasers and all the rest of the paraphernalia in use in faraway Kandahar in 2010. I am also sure his modern counterparts would be proud to carry forward the legacy of excellence earned by him and his comrades.

Ubique!

Brian Reid
October 2010

Introduction

After three years of all-out warfare, the Allies had little to encourage them from their earlier operations against the German Imperial Army on the Western Front. The Germans, on the other hand, had been able to retain most of the territory they had gained in the autumn of 1914.

The Russian Revolution had undermined the morale and discipline of its armies, leading to a collapse of their resistance against the Central Powers. The Central Powers commanded the German Imperial Army as well as the considerable assets of the Austro-Hungarian Empire. Although the German armies had to maintain a significant presence in the East to ensure that there would be no resurgence of the Russian military forces, they were able to release many divisions to fight on the Western Front.

The Allies were slowly building up their strength in men and materials but they could not match the immediate build-up of the German forces as they rapidly brought battle-hardened troops, fresh from their successes in the East, to the Western Front. However, although the German Imperial Army was able temporarily to outnumber the Allies at any point of concentration, this advantage could not be sustained over many months in view of the growing resources becoming available to the Allies from the USA. It was therefore vital, as far as General Ludendorff was concerned, for the German attack to be launched as soon as the spring weather in 1918 and their build-up of forces would permit. It was potentially a war-winning strategy if they could reach the English Channel, but even so, the German High Command was conscious that should they not prevail, the war would be lost.

Some of the most successful fighting troops on the Western Front, proven by their remarkable track record at Vimy Ridge, Hill 70 and Passchendaele, were those of the Canadian Corps. Their four divisions had shown in every engagement that they were more than a match for the German forces pitted against them. The Allied High Command had often turned to the Canadians when they needed to ensure a successful outcome against the odds. They had become, though not by their own choice, the storm troops of the British armies on the Western Front.

The reasons for their military success were to be found not only in the innate courage and toughness of men brought up to live and work in Canada's severe weather conditions, but also in their organisation and training. They also came from a pioneering environment that allowed and rewarded individual initiative and enterprise. Their Commander-in-Chief, Lieutenant General Sir Arthur Currie, strongly believed in the power of his artillery in assisting the infantry to overcome enemy resistance. He had encouraged the field artillery to train their gunners to maintain fire on enemy emplacements during an infantry assault, so that the advancing infantrymen could be confident while moving forward. The speed of a creeping barrage could be controlled accurately enough for the infantry

'Capture of Vimy Ridge: 1917. The Guns Move Up.' A watercolour sketch by 'J.C.W.' with the following annotations: 'Albain St. Nazaire below in the middle distance. Bois de Buvigny behind. Clarency in middle background.' (*Courtesy of the Woolwich Artillery Museum*)

to overcome the enemy as soon as the line of shell fire moved on; close liaison between the artillery and infantry commanders made this a matter of routine. These tactics were first used by the Canadians at Vimy Ridge, where the infantry and field artillery were trained to coordinate closely their advance.

The most significant development in the organisation of the Canadian Artillery was undoubtedly the formation of the Counter Battery Staff Office (CBSO), headed by Lieutenant Colonel Andrew McNaughton. This office gradually took charge of the tactics employed by heavy and field artillery in the planned destruction of enemy batteries. McNaughton was an electrical engineering graduate of McGill University and his post-graduate work had made him familiar with the use of the newly invented oscillographs. A team of British scientists, including the Nobel Prize winner Lawrence Bragg, had been sent to carry out field trials of these instruments, working with the Canadians, who took up their ideas with enthusiasm.

Sound ranging was a new and improved method for identifying the location and calibre of enemy guns – more effective in most cases than flash spotting. Sound ranging used lines of sensitive microphones located behind the front lines, forming a sound ranging base from which accurate enemy gun locations could be determined. These microphones were linked to an oscillograph, on which each showed a trace with a blip when a sound was recorded. By being able to record accurately, using a series of pens on a roll of paper, the time difference between the blips from the different microphones for the same gun, the Canadians were able to determine the positions of the German batteries even when they were out of sight. Despite many teething troubles, this technique was becoming a practical reality early in 1917 and had soon evolved to reveal the types and calibre of guns, the size of batteries and other related information. Furthermore, McNaughton devised a management system using intelligence frequently and rapidly updated from sound ranging, flash spotting, and aerial and ground observation. This provided the Canadian Artillery with accurate maps showing the locations of enemy batteries and helped them determine the best ways of destroying these batteries.

By the time the battle for Vimy Ridge was successfully fought in April 1917, the Canadians were able to knock out 60 per cent of the opposing artillery in the weeks before their troops began to advance. Because they were confident of being able to withhold their fire on certain batteries until just before the battle, the enemy was denied the time necessary to bring up replacements. There is no doubt that had they done so, surviving enemy artillery could have wrought havoc in the Canadian infantry as they took on the well-defended positions facing them on the steep slopes of the ridge.

Heavy trench mortars became regarded as forward artillery, under their own command, liaising closely with the infantry. Improvements in the mountings of the heavy Newton trench mortars, making them more mobile and accurate, were to be continuously developed for the battles of 1918. Machine-gun battalions were organised and fully trained as units under their own command; some were mounted on trucks and light-tracked vehicles in order to keep up with rapidly moving infantry. These units came to be regarded as a branch of artillery and were particularly useful during assaults and in the defence of vital strong points against advancing enemy infantry.

Tank formations, although none were on the nominal strength of the Canadian Corps, were sometimes placed under their command when the situation required them. The tactical use of tanks was first proven at the Battle of Cambrai in 1917, although their mechanical reliability under battle conditions was frequently questioned. Tanks were first used as cavalry-type support in the Canadian assaults in the opening phases of the Battle of Amiens, and then in the battles that followed later in the autumn of 1918.

All of these arrangements gave the Canadian infantry uniquely strong and coordinated support, both to resist enemy attacks, and to give them greater confidence when they were called upon to assault enemy positions.

In October and November 1917, all four Canadian divisions had been employed in overcoming German resistance at Passchendaele. It had been the most demanding battle of the war so far for the Canadians, fought in atrocious weather and ground conditions. The Canadians had to attack uphill against entrenched enemy positions and well-sited machine-gun emplacements in concrete pillboxes right across the slopes. It was unsurprising that by the time they were relieved, having taken Passchendaele Ridge and set up a defendable perimeter, they had suffered 15,600 battlefield casualties out of a total strength of about 100,000 troops employed.

Most of the replacements for the casualties incurred in the latter part of 1917 had to be drawn from the men who had been recruited to form two further Canadian divisions. For a time, this had been a source of contention between the commanders in the field and the political leaders, who had come to believe that two further divisions would enhance Canadian influence in the British High Command. General Currie was able to win the arguments against the formation of new divisions and, supported by his field commanders, to make better use of the resources thus released. However, he agreed to form a fifth Canadian Divisional Artillery group, which was to play an important role as part of the Canadian Corps.

Major Arthur Hardie Bick, who had commanded the 15th Battery CFA during the battles of Hill 70 and Passchendaele, took up the post of Brigade

Arthur Hardie Bick at his graduation in Mining Engineering (MA) from Queens University, Kingston, in 1912.

Major of the 1st Canadian Divisional Artillery in December 1917. As one of his duties, he wrote the daily war diaries for his division from 21 December 1917. They are more or less continuously handwritten by him, apart from brief absences, until February 1919. Major Bick had trained as a member of the Canadian Militia from 1909 onwards while he was studying mining and civil engineering at Queen's University. He won distinction both as a marksman and as a signaller before being commissioned in June 1912. He joined the first contingent of the Canadian Expeditionary Force (CEF) prior to its embarkation for England in September 1914, serving in the Canadian Field Artillery (CFA) throughout the war, apart from a period of six months spent recovering from wounds sustained at the Second Battle of Ypres.

The diaries have been set out in separate chapters covering the main phases of the battles of 1918. Commentaries have been included, informed mainly by the Interim Report 'Canadian Corps Operations During the Year 1918'. That report had been written by Lieutenant General Sir A. W. Currie shortly after the end of hostilities. Maps derived from it have also been included to show dispositions in the battlefields where the Canadian Corps fought. Other texts consulted have been listed in the bibliography and a glossary has been included to explain the meaning and context of unusual words and initials used by Major Bick in his diaries. The transcribed diary text has been indented and a slightly smaller font has been used. The diary entry for each day begins with the location of the headquarters where it was written, the date and a short report on the weather conditions as they affected artillery operations.

The diaries begin in December 1917 and end in February 1919. The Canadian Corps played a decisive role in these months. Beginning with the anxious preparations in anticipation of a great German offensive, the diaries show how the unique effectiveness of the artillery was brought to bear. Each chapter describes how the four Canadian divisions were employed as spearheads to overcome the defensive military systems built up by the Germans over the first three years of the war.

CHAPTER ONE

Preparing to Meet the German Onslaught

21 December 1917 – 20 March 1918

Following their success in the battle for Passchendaele, the four divisions of the Canadian Corps had been resting behind the lines for several weeks. The diaries open with the Corps' first deployment on the fighting front north of Arras. At this stage there were still severe shortages of both officers and men due to the casualties they had suffered during their most recent engagement. Replacements were being brought over from the Canadian contingents already based in England. Before the battle, a group of powerful Canadian politicians had hoped to form two further divisions to bring the fighting strength of Canadian Forces in the field to six divisions. Thus, it would have enabled Canada to field two Canadian Corps, each with three divisions. Such an arrangement was strongly opposed by field commanders, but at this stage it remained an objective thanks to political support.

Initially, General Currie detailed two divisions, the 3rd and 4th, to hold the front, with the 1st and 2nd in reserve to continue with the training of replacements arriving from England. He planned to rotate the divisions regularly with two holding the front at all times.

Major Bick, having commanded the 15th Battery during the Battle of Passchendaele, had been posted to take over as Acting Brigade Major of the 1st Canadian Divisional Artillery while Major D. A. White went on leave. However, owing to the shortage of experienced officers, he remained on the strength of the 15th Battery. His second-in-command, Captain B. B. McConkey MC, took over in his absence at Divisional Headquarters.

During the anxious time throughout the winter months, while the Germans were preparing to attack, the Canadians were far from idle.

Major Arthur Hardie Bick, Brigade Major 1st Canadian Divisional Artillery, April 1918 – February 1919.

The Canadian Corps was responsible for a front facing the enemy from Hill 70 to Mericourt. The divisions were deployed and rotated with two at the front and two in reserve to rest and undergo further training in mobile warfare. Behind them was the now even more formidable fortress of Vimy Ridge. It was vital to defend the remainder of the French coalfields, many of them being already in enemy hands, and the Canadians adopted a strategy of aggressive defence. They were to harass the enemy along its front by bombarding its rear areas to make any troops assembling there as uncomfortable as possible. Furthermore, by defining SOS lines and registering field and heavy artillery just beyond them, the Canadians could focus the full weight of their artillery batteries on sensitive spots where the enemy appeared to be preparing to raid or make massed assaults.

------ooo------

Diaries for December 1917

The diaries written by Major Bick open on 21 December 1917.

BRUAY Dec/21. Fine and cold. Visibility fair at times.

Headquarters 1st CDA moved at 10am from CHATEAU DE LA HAIE to CHATEAU between BRUAY and DIVION. Remainder of 1st Brigade and relieved TM personnel moved to MARLES-LES-MINES and BRUAY respectively.

3 casualties resulted in 1st Bde CFA due to horses falling on slippery roads – none fatal. Issued notes on training.

Allied air power by now predominated in the daylight hours, but in the half light, when visual interceptions by allied fighters would have been difficult, German bombers could roam at will over the allied lines and rear areas to bomb targets of opportunity.

BRUAY Dec/22. Dull and a little milder.

1st Brigade settled in MARLES-LES-MINES. Men's billets on the whole only fair. Horses in one battery under cover ... rest of brigade in brickfields and fields.

BETHUNE heavily bombed about 5pm. 1st Divisional car had narrow escape.

BRUAY Dec/23. Dull and very cold.

BETHUNE bombed at dusk for 20 minutes. ADD#1 to o.o.50 issued.

13-pdr anti-aircraft guns. (*Courtesy of the RCA Museum*)

'Snow fell in time to provide a seasonable Canadian setting for Christmas day. In the rest areas some batteries sat down in one of the estaminets to a dinner worthy of the occasion; others enjoyed the festive meal in their billets. Big Canadian mails had been arriving, and there was no lack of fruit cake, nuts, raisins and other Christmas delicacies.' Nicholson, *Gunners of Canada*.

BRUAY Dec/24. Milder, fine rain at intervals. Visibility poor.

One section per battery relieved of 2nd Brigade and withdrawn to wagon lines ABLAIN ST. NAZAIRE.

All preparations for Xmas dinners being completed by Hdqrs 1st Brigade and part of Trench Mortars.

BRUAY Dec/25. Very Mild.

1 Section per battery 2nd Brigade marched to wagon lines HALLICOURT. 2nd Brigade relief in the line completed.

A posed photograph of a 60-pdr being loaded. 'A busting time this Christmas' is written on the shell. (*Courtesy of the RCA Museum*)

Heavy snow storm commenced 7pm. Thaw precautions in force as from 8pm.
Headquarters dinner held in school, BRUAY at 6pm with huge success.
Orders are 1st Canadian Division are Corps reserve; to move on 6 hours notice.

The festivities have led to one tragic event in the death of a Canadian gunner in connection with which an enquiry was to be held. Deployments still had to be made in response to the anticipated resumption of more active hostilities.

BRUAY Dec/26. Dull and cold.

2nd Brigade completed march to HALLICOURT. No casualties resulted although roads were very glase.
Gnr Bayley 5th Battery was shot and killed by French civilian in GOUY-SERVINS during Christmas night.

Major White returns from leave and, since he is being posted to a senior job in Canadian Corps Headquarters, this leaves Major Bick to continue as Acting Brigade Major of 1st CDA. The commander of 1st CDA, Brigadier General H. C. Thacker, referred to as the CRA, resumes his inspection routines in the aftermath of Christmas.

BRUAY Dec/27. Cold and misty.

Informal inspection made by CRA of 2nd Brigade lines in HALLICOURT during morning. Court of Enquiry ordered on BAYLEY Case in 2nd Brigade.

Major D A White returns from leave and goes to Corps as S.O.R.A.

Gas lecture and trials under Div. Gas Officer at BRUAY THEATRE from 10am to 1pm.

BRUAY Dec/28. Dull and very cold. Ground remains covered with snow.

On inspection billets at HALLICOURT were found in bad condition and inadequate.

BRUAY Dec/29. Misty and very cold. Roads very glase. Ground snow covered.

Lt Col Anderson assumes temp command of 1st Div. Arty. while Brig Gen Thacker is on English leave. Lieut J H McLaren proceeds on infantry course Boulogne.

Training continues, but the Germans are evidently resuming more active hostilities. Taking advantage of weather conditions thought to be favourable to the use of projectors, the enemy launches a gas attack, but with very little effect on the Canadians.

BRUAY Dec/30. Mild. Roads very slippery. Snow still remains.

Lieuts Mathewson and Lepper Trench Mortar Battery and 6 men proceed to gas school COUPIGNY for week course. 30 remounts received from base.

Enemy used Gas Projectors against Canadians for first time this morning with very few casualties resulting.

BRUAY Dec/31. Dull and windy. Very cold. Roads very slippery. Snow.

Canadian Corps Defence Scheme APPENDIX 1– "Artillery" received.

45 NCOs sent to Can Corps Artillery School PERNES which opens Jan 2nd. Lieut McLean 1st CDAC and 4 NCOs proceed to ABBEVILLE for Veterinary Course.

Diaries for January 1918

The last months of 1917 saw the release of large contingents of the German Imperial Army for deployment on the Western Front – a consequence of the Russian collapse in the East. It allowed the Germans to outnumber the Allies wherever they wished, enabling them to choose to their best advantage where to begin their spring offensive.

General Douglas Haig, Commander-in-Chief of British Forces, stated that 'We must be prepared to meet a strong and sustained hostile attack'. The Canadian Corps were holding a 7-mile front from Acheville to Loos as shown in Map 1. General Currie, commander of the Canadian Corps, decided at this stage to place two of his four divisions in the line (at the front), with two divisions held in reserve. He also strongly advocated using the latest contingents of troops arriving from Canada as replacements and reinforcements for the four divisions in France rather than attempting to form two further divisions, the 5th and 6th, in anticipation of forming two Canadian Corps, each consisting of three divisions. His proposals were at first met with equally strong representations from those not so closely concerned with the fighting in the field. Currie argued that casualty rates so far had shown that even with conscription (recently introduced in Canada) it would be impossible to provide replacements to maintain even one further division up to strength.

The British forces were also under pressure to keep their units up to strength at the front. In order to do this they had been persuaded to reduce the number of infantry battalions to three per brigade rather than four. Currie, however, put forward his arguments for strengthening the infantry battalions. He believed that each battalion should have one hundred extra men, the men who would otherwise have formed elements of the two new divisions being planned by Canadian politicians. Currie finally won agreement to his plan, thereby ensuring that the Canadian Corps would continue to supply the most formidable allied formations. Canadian infantry brigades were each able to retain a strength of four battalions compared to the three attributed to brigades in other branches of the British Army.

The divisions of the Canadian Corps and their support groups had evolved to be much stronger than their British counterparts. There were three battalions of engineers and enhanced medical and logistics teams in each division, making them self-supporting in many ways. However, Currie strongly preferred to keep all four divisions operating as a team with the support of the staff organisation at Corps HQ. The coordination of artillery operations, of the five divisional artillery groups as well as their heavy artillery, through the CBSO was particularly important.

The New Year opened with the 1st CDA still in reserve, concentrating on the training of men for replacement at the front and the improvement

An 18-pdr on a firing platform. (*Courtesy of the RCA Museum*)

of their equipment. But now there was more emphasis on plans for flexible defensive tactics because of the possibility of a breakthrough by the enemy.

BRUAY Jan/1. Dull and Cold. Roads glase. Snow on Ground.

No Training in 2nd Bde. Owing to delayed Xmas festivities being held.

One 18 pdr with AIR RECUPERATOR sent to TRAINING Battery Canadian Artillery School, PERNES.

Among 'MENTIONS' in HAIG's Despatch Nov. 7. Brig Gen H C THACKER C.M.G., Major F J ALDERSON, MAJOR A T MACKAY, MAJOR C V STOCKWELL, MAJOR H T C WHITLEY, Lt C B BELK, CAPT. R H DEAN, LT W H LEISHMAN, LT W R SKEY.

Although the 1st Canadian Division is in reserve and therefore not directly involved, enemy raids on the troops holding the front are increasing. However, the 1st Division will be moving up when their turn comes. The artillery will have to be quick to respond rapidly to urgent SOS calls to defend infantry in the line.

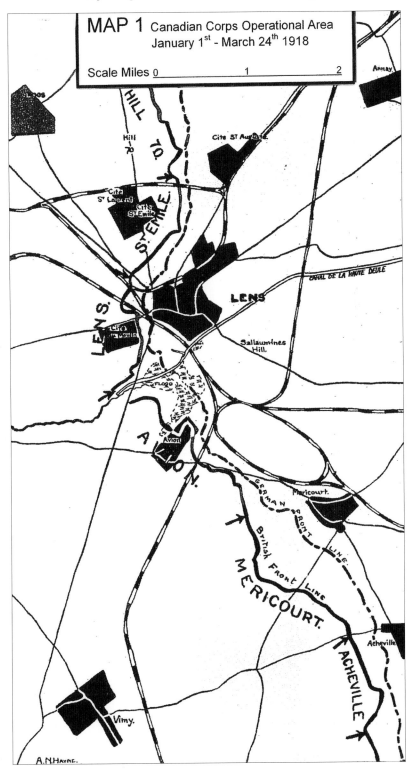

Canadian Corps' Operational Area, 1 January to 24 March 1918.

BRUAY Jan/2. Mild. Roads wet and icy. Snow still covers ground.

Training in Machine Gunnery is commenced in 1st and 2nd Brigades.

Can. Corps front raided at three points during last night which points to increased uneasiness of the enemy.

Training generally is slow owing to great shortage in Officers and NCOs – on leave and on courses.

BRUAY Jan/3. Rain about 1am. Fair and cold during daylight. Roads very icy. Some snow remains.

Two DSOs in the gazette MAJOR C V STOCKWELL 4th Bty CFA [Canadian Field Artillery], MAJOR F J ALDERSON 5th Bty CFA.

MAP showing Left Reinforcement Scheme and APPENDIX (Assembly Positions) issued. Capt K BOVILL 1st Bde. [Brigade] assumes temporary duties of Staff Captain 1st CDA. [1st Canadian Divisional Artillery]

MAJOR H T WHITLEY struck off strength and posted thru Pt II Orders to Reserve Artillery WITLEY Eng.

BRUAY Jan/4. Very cold and slightly misty. Roads icy. Snow remains.

Very quiet. Training carried on as usual.

Two MCs in the Gazette MAJOR W G HANSON 7th Bty CFA and Lieut LG Black 1st CDTMG.

BRUAY Jan/5. Milder. Misty. Roads wet and icy.

Temporary Preliminary Measures received from 1st Div for Reinforcing Corps Front. Assembly Places for Artillery are not considered suitable. Suggested that points covered in our Temporary Reinforcing Orders of the 3rd be adopted.

MAJOR F J ALDERSON leaves for 3 months in Canada.

BRUAY Jan/6. Extremely cold. Visibility very fair. Roads icy. Snow remains.

Two DCMs in New Years Gazette. #40164 BSM S C EVANS (now RSM 1st Bde CFA), #41176 BSM A K McDONALD 6th Bty CFA.

Assembly Areas for LEFT Division Front are now NOEUX – LES – MINES and BRAQUEMONT. Routes to these areas and also to possible Assembly area at VIMY RIDGE via AIX NOULETTE, SOUCHEZ are still being questioned. Milder at dusk with rain.

BRUAY Jan/7. Very mild. Rain thru out the night. Slightly misty. Roads becoming muddy.

Temporary Reinforcement Measures issued on 3rd inst cancelled and Appendices 'A', 'B' and 'C' of REINFORCEMENT SCHEME issued.

Lecture on Air Recuperator at 2nd Bde CFM HALLICOURT by T.O.M. Southern Section First Army was very successful.

BRUAY Jan/8. Fair and cold in early morning. Heavy fall of snow 9 – 11am. Roads in bad shape.

Appendix "Aa" and Addendas #1 to Apps "B" and "C" of REINFORCEMENT SCHEME issued.

1st Brigade CFA visited and found to be in good shape except one battery. Horses in good condition. Steel and harness in three batteries very fair.

BRUAY Jan/9. Fair and cold in early morning changing to snow and wind later in the day. Roads in fair shape.

MAJ. GEN. A C MacDONELL GOC 1st Can. Div. began inspection of 1st Div. Arty. 1st Bty and 2nd Bty of 1st Brigade, and 5th Bty and 6th Bty of 2nd Brigade CFA were inspected. All batteries were in fair shape and "great improvement on last inspection" shown. Conditions for inspecting were extremely bad in the afternoon at 2nd Brigade.

Warning Order for Relief of 3rd CDA received.

Instructions are received from Corps HQ giving almost two weeks' notice for the 1st Canadian Division to relieve the 3rd Canadian Division at the front.

BRUAY Jan/10. Snow almost entirely disappeared. Roads very icy.

Reinforcing Scheme issued for reinforcing either Divisional Front. Issued Warning Order for relief on night 23/24 January.

Visit made to 1st Army School of Mines, HOUCHIN. Course was found very instructive and supplies apparently proper methods to be adopted in Dug-Out Construction as was seen by the work done.

MAJOR H T C WHITLEY returns from O/S Course and knows nothing of his transfer to Reserve Artillery in England.

BRUAY Jan/11. Very mild. Roads wet and muddy. Visibility fair. Snow entirely disappeared.

All battery commanders of two brigades left at 7.30am for reconnaissance of support positions on Left Division Sector and also to reconnoiter their prospective battery positions to be occupied on relief of 3rd CDA about 23/24 January.

THAW conditions prevail at midnight 11/12 January.

BRUAY Jan/12. Mild. Very cool wind. Visibility fair. Roads very muddy.

Issued ADDENDA #2 to App "C" Reinforcing Scheme relating to actual reinforcing positions on Left Division Front.

Lieut H H Blake R.O. 1st CDA proceeded by leave train to BOULOGNE to report on conditions of journey.

BRUAY Jan/13. Fine and clear. Frost enough during night to make roads very good.

Lieut Col J G PIERCY 1st Bde proceeds to England on leave: MAJOR A A DURKEE taking over command. Brig Gen THACKER returns from leave.

BRUAY Jan/14. Dull and mild. Snow fell during the night. Roads in very bad shape.

C.R.A. visits batteries and Hdqrs 1st Bde CFA MARLES-LES-MINES.

MAJOR H T WHITLEY goes to hospital.

1st Brigade [CFA] are deficient several senior officers. Actually available for duty – 1 Major, 1 Captain, 2 Acting Captains.

Relief Orders received from Division. Front will have 1st, 3rd and 5th DTM Groups when 1st Div take over command.

BRUAY Jan/15. Mild and windy. Visibility poor. Snow disappeared. Roads very muddy. Rain thru out the day.

Water from stream rose very rapidly towards dusk and at 10pm was level with the floor of office of CRA.

BRUAY Jan/16. Very windy. Mild. Roads hard but muddy. Impossible to reach 1st CDA Hdqrs Office without going thru 3 feet of water.

Office moved to BRUAY town. Lieut BLAKE R.O. 1st CDA proceeds on leave to England.

BRUAY Jan/17. Dull and very wet. Thaw conditions in force. Roads very bad.

2nd Bde began rifle shooting at BOIS DES DAMES Rifle Range but had to stop owing to the rain.

Lecture at Div Hdqrs by GSO1 Col PARSONS as to General Intention on going into the line.

BRUAY Jan/18. Dull. Roads very wet.

Rifle practice carried on by 2nd Brigade.

Reconnaissance of positions on HILL 70 and ST EMILE Sectors made. It is decided by CRA to hold the front: by taking two 18 pdr Batteries from 5th CDA holding ST EMILE Front giving ST EMILE 4 – 18pdrs 2 – How's. Grouping of batteries will be Left Group, Centre Group, Right Group covering Left Battalion HILL 70, Right Battalion HILL 70, ST EMILE Sectors respectively.

BRUAY Jan/19. Dull. Roads in bad condition. Thaw conditions still in force.

Rifle practice at BOIS DES DAMES by 2nd Bde, 1st CDTM Brigade [CFA] and 1st Brigade.

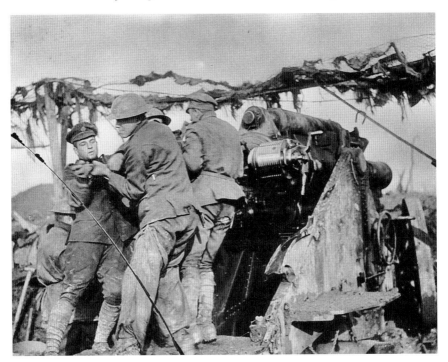

A 9.2-inch Howitzer with gun crew. (*Courtesy of the RCA Museum*)

Conference of General Officers held at Corps to meet Overseas Minister of Militia.

5th Battery made reconnaissance of FOSSE 7 de BETHUNE and found suitable battery position. Officers from 3rd CDA HQs made reconnaissance of BRUAY area lines.

Issued Operational Order for the relief of 3rd CDA.

BRUAY Jan/20. Mild. Visibility very poor. Thaw conditions still in force.

Rifle practice at BOIS DES DAMES being completed by 1st Brigade CFA.

Capt DEAN makes report on reconnaissance of HILL 70 Front Trench Mortar positions. Policy decided is that 3rd CDA TMs continue working as at present. 1st CDA TMs will build new positions on reverse slope of HILL 70 for 4 Medium and 2 Heavy Trench Mortars.

Issued to units concerned the intention of the 1st CDA regarding grouping of artillery on HILL 70 and ST EMILE Sectors shortly following the relief of 3rd CDA.

BRUAY Jan/21. Mild. Raining slightly. Visibility very poor.

GOC 1st Can. Div. inspected 48th Howitzer Battery at HALLICOURT lines. Battery was found in very fair shape. GRO received regarding transfer of guns shipped.

Sanction of GOCRA received to have relief of 3rd CDA continue in accordance with GRO#2750 – Guns handed over complete in sights, tools and spare parts.

BRUAY Jan/22. Mild. Slight rain. Roads very wet and bad condition owing to thaw.

GOC 1st Can Division inspected 7th Battery. Battery in very fair shape.

5th Battery moved to Wagon Lines near BRAQUEMONT. New position being occupied at Fosse 7 de BETHUNE.

One section moves in night 22/23. All remaining batteries relieve one section of 3rd CD in the line.

CRA visited Canadian Corps Artillery School at PERNES.

BRUAY Jan/23. Very mild. Roads in muddy condition.

CRA inspects the two brigades on line of march. 2nd Brigade CFA was in very good shape. Steelwork almost entirely burnished.

Relief of all batteries and brigades carried out.

The relief completed, enemy activity begins to take effect. The disposition of artillery is of great importance, particularly in relation to Hill 70. The successful assault on Hill 70 by the Canadians after the Battle of Vimy Ridge in 1917 has given them a commanding position overlooking the surrounding area. Now the heavily fortified ridge immediately behind them completes a very strong defensive system, developed to resist enemy assaults during the anticipated offensive.

BRUAY Jan/24. Mild. Roads in fair condition. Visibility fair.

CRA takes over command of HILL 70 and St EMILE sectors at 10am from CRA 3rd CDA.

Guns of 5th Battery found to be very bad especially from their position at FOSSE 7 de BETHUNE.

Front quiet except for shelling of LOOS area.

Divisional Artillery Hdqrs moved from BRUAY to BRAQUEMONT (125 Rue NATIONALE).

Enemy counter batteries are taking their first toll of casualties in the 1st CDA Field Artillery. Their increased use of aircraft for bombing and infantry for raiding is having limited success. Four men are taken prisoner by them during a raid.

BRAQUEMONT Jan/25. Very mild. Visibility very fair.

General Staff advise Tank Gun put on HILL 70 north of NESTOR Trench would suit requirements for anti Tank defence on central portion of Divisional Front.

Shelling of 1st Battery position in ST PIERRE. 1 Sergeant killed, 3 wounded.

Bombs dropped on 5th CDA Batteries in M22. HERSIN registered by moonlight and shelled from 7.30pm – 10.30pm.

Raid at 6am at NORMAN STACKS, 4 men missing.

BRAQUEMONT Jan/26. Fine. Visibility poor except for one hour in afternoon. Very quiet day.

T.Ms active on HILL 70 Supports for short period.

CRA visits DAC at HOUCHIN.

Artillery support is now being referred to as Left, Center and Right Groups to simplify fire instructions when supporting infantry in the line.

BRAQUEMONT Jan/27. Fine. Visibility poor.

Hostile artillery exceptionally quiet.

Authority obtained for using LEFT Group How. Battery for general work.

In spite of the fact that night was quite bright and that it is the Kaiser's birthday no shelling or bombing has taken place.

A 12-inch Howitzer in a camouflaged position. (*Courtesy of the RCA Museum*)

BRAQUEMONT Jan/28. Fine. Visibility poor in morning – fair in the afternoon.

Slight increase in hostile artillery. Shelling of LIEVIN and FOSSE 7 de BETHUNE.

Hostile T.M. only slightly active.

Fair progress being made in wiring and strengthening of battery positions.

Pigeon Service is being used with success as a means of communication.

BRAQUEMONT Jan/29. Fine. Visibility fair at times. Slight frost thru out night.

6th Battery position at LOOS was shelled by 4.1 from 9.30am to 2.30pm. 2 guns slightly damaged, no personnel.

Pigeon messages are being received 30 minutes after despatch from Group Hdqrs.

Enemy aircraft very active during day and night.

BRAQUEMONT Jan/30. Fair and mild. Slightly misty. Visibility poor owing to heavy ground mist.

CRA visits Centre Group Batteries. Good impression given especially by the keenness of all ranks in building and repair work being done in the GUN area. Defence scheme issued.

BRAQUEMONT Jan/31. Fair and mild. Slightly misty. Visibility poor owing to heavy ground mist.

Front very quiet all day.

Diaries for February 1918

The 1st Division Artillery, having recovered from their part in the Passchendaele battle, was engaging with the enemy again. The Germans had become quite active in harassing rear areas and spasmodically raiding the troop formations in the line. Also, enemy air activity, which discouraged the use of observation balloons, had increased significantly. The forward artillery Observation Posts (OPs) were therefore vital in keeping track of enemy movements and spotting the fall of shot as the Canadian Artillery harassed their preparations for an offensive. However, experience was to reveal the vulnerability of OPs due to their exposed positions and the difficulty of concealing them effectively from enemy observation.

There was a great deal of enemy activity behind the lines, both in building up their forces and improving road and rail communications. But concealment in the numerous towns and small villages not far behind their lines made it difficult to see much of enemy troop concentrations.

However, there was no doubt whatsoever that the build-up was continuing and the forthcoming assault could be concentrated anywhere along the broad front defended by the Allies. It was certain to be very strong indeed and likely to break through Allied defences in some places.

Schemes for defence in depth were implemented. The artillery brigades planned to be able to move their guns into successive defensive positions should a breakthrough take place. The dominating high ground, especially around Hill 70 and Vimy Ridge, was being thoroughly prepared. There were many new field- and machine-gun emplacements well defended by wire and accessed by tunnels. The area behind Vimy Ridge was strategically important because many coal mines remaining in Allied hands were located there. The area south and east of Vimy was also to be defended in depth, with plans to inundate the flood plain of the Scarpe River by constructing dams to control its flow should the need arise.

The reorganisation of the Canadian Divisions currently underway was to make much better use of trench mortars and machine guns. These were easier to move than the heavier field guns in response to enemy threats. Field gun positions, being more permanent, had to be carefully camouflaged and, wherever possible, made invulnerable against counter battery fire from the enemy.

BRAQUEMONT Feb/1. Fine and cool. Frost at night. Visibility very poor owing to ground mist.

Front extremely quiet. CRA visits positions of RIGHT GROUP. All ranks show great interest and keenness in getting "wired in" and getting positions 5.9 proof.

BRAQUEMONT Feb/2. Fine and cool. Frost at night. Visibility poor at times. Roads become very muddy.

Front very quiet. Policy of using TMs instead of 4.5 How's on all targets in enemy Front Line system and for retaliation is introduced.

BRAQUEMONT Feb/3. Fine and cool. Frost at night. Visibility fair.

Hostile TMs active during early morning and at odd intervals thru out the day.

Enemy raiding parties were difficult to detect in advance but sometimes, as in the case below, evidence of their intention had been given by the results of wire-cutting expeditions. It was relatively straightforward for fire to be directed promptly when an enemy raid began.

BRAQUEMONT Feb/4. Fine Weather. Visibility poor but fair at times.

A 6-inch Howitzer firing. (*Courtesy of the RCA Museum*)

Suggested TM emplacements off HYTHE TUNNEL are reconnoitered and deemed OK by DTMO. Suggested that ANTI-TANK GUN be placed near the TUNNEL on HILL 70.

Two lanes found cut in our wire in H32d near GRAVEL PIT. Extra 6" How and TM protection arranged.

BRAQUEMONT Feb/5. Fine and cool Visibility fair.

Much movement is reported in enemy lines. Relief of Division opposite suspected.

ST EMILE Sector raided at two points by 3rd Battn at 7.44pm. Result is very unfavorable – no prisoners taken. Succession of failures by STEALTH RAIDS will probably result in their being forbidden in the future.

Local small-scale raids made by the Canadian infantry are clearly not a success. However, it is important that enemy troops in the trenches and positions should be harassed and prisoners taken to provide up-to-date intelligence. This was sometimes problematic because the Germans habitually maintained only a skeleton manning of the forward trenches with fighting units positioned further back until they were required to attack.

The enemy was making similar raiding efforts but with a similar lack of success. The future policy of the Canadian Corps was to make carefully planned raids on a much larger scale. Such raids would have to penetrate further to the rear of the enemy positions if they were to be successful.

BRAQUEMONT Feb/6. Fair Weather. Visibility fair at odd intervals.

CRA visits positions of LEFT GROUP.

Preparations are being made for large raid on LEFT Infantry Brigade. Lecture on Heavy Artillery at HOUDAIN by GSO1 Artillery 1st Army.

Enemy attempted to raid our trenches at NORMAN STACKS but was unsuccessful. Artillery protection opened up very quickly.

Artillery promotion list is sent out for information from Corps.

BRAQUEMONT Feb/7. Fine weather. Visibility fair at times but mist which has prevented good observation for past two weeks still prevails.

TMs begin wire cutting for raid by 3rd Can. Inf. Brigade. On HILL 70 Sector.

Abnormal train movement towards south is reported by Artillery OPs on HILL 70.

BRAQUEMONT Feb/8. Dull and rain. Visibility poor.

Arrangements for HILL 70 Raid are progressing slowly.

BRAQUEMONT Feb/9. Fair and mild. Visibility good.

Scattered shelling over whole area.

Artillery arrangements made for the raid on HILL 70 Section by CRA after conferring with CRA 11th Div Artillery and Centre and Left Group Commanders.

The use of heavy-calibre trench mortars (6-inch Newtons) was problematic, and attempts to stabilise them during continuous operation were unsatisfactory. In order to make them easier to move, some changes were made to lighten and strengthen their installations.

BRAQUEMONT Feb/10. Fine and windy. Visibility poor in morning and good in afternoon.

Wire cutting progresses on HILL 70 Front.

Trench Mortars are experiencing great difficulty in keeping guns in action owing to breaking of guys traversing and elevating. Supply of these guys or struts must be increased as over 50% of TM 6" Newtons is out of action each day due to the above-named cause.

Preparation for a major raid on enemy trenches is proving to be very time-consuming and the commander of the Canadian Infantry Brigade (GOC, CIB) requests howitzers to help with wire cutting.

BRAQUEMONT Feb/11. Dull weather. Very windy.

CRA makes tour of OPs during the morning.

GOC C.I.B orders 6" Howitzers to help out on wire cutting. Intention is that raid should take place at 3am February 12th. Gaps reported cut by Light Stokes were found by patrols to be impassable. Delay of 24 hours ordered as gaps are not cut. Front remains quiet.

A 9.2-inch Howitzer moving into cover. (*Courtesy of the RCA Museum*)

BRAQUEMONT Feb/12. Mild. Visibility poor.

GOC 3rd CIB wishes artillery now to cut all remaining wire.

Trench Mortars and Artillery cut wire all day. Infantry express satisfaction with gaps D and E near NORMAN STACKS but later claim that Gap E is not passable.

Raid is ordered for 3am tomorrow. Front is normally quiet.

The raid first mooted on 6 February finally takes place. It goes well enough and it achieves all its objectives. However, enemy artillery came into action in response.

BRAQUEMONT Feb/13. Rain and mist. Visibility poor.

Raid on HILL 70 Front at 3am. Enemy retaliation late in starting. Very heavy enemy barrage of 77s, 4.1s and 5.9s at 3.20am on supports.

Enemy fire died away after our fire stopped at 3.46am and finally stopped at 3.54am. Southern gap near NORMAN STACKS was not attempted. Parties were able to penetrate into enemy Front Line at two northern gaps capturing 6 prisoners of 220th Division (normal) and 2 machine guns.

Front quiet all day. 4th Canadian Division ask for cooperation in raid on trenches before LENS tomorrow morning.

Despite some increase in gas shelling by the enemy, ceremonials are being observed. Belgian decorations are presented at Canadian Corps HQ and there is a reunion dinner for all original 1st Division Officers at the Canadian Corps Club.

BRAQUEMONT Feb/14. Mild. Visibility very poor. Misty. Front quiet.

Increase in gas shelling over battery areas at night.

Division on our right captured a post in raid at 5.45am. Our Right Group cooperated for 6 minutes.

Presentation of Belgian decorations made at Corps Headquarters COMBLAIN L'ABBÉ at 11am by Army Commander.

Dinner of reunion of all original 1st Division officers held at club Can. Corps – over 100 attended.

Work on defensive positions with fall back situations progresses with urgency. This is clearly the priority over all other types of activity at present.

BRAQUEMONT Feb/15. Chilly weather. Visibility poor. Front normally quiet.

All Defensive positions visited and generally found OK – few changes of locations being necessitated. Work on RED LINE Areas is being rushed with all possible speed. All units are very short of men for ordinary routine work due to large working parties employed.

BRAQUEMONT Feb/16. Very cool. Visibility good in morning but only fair in afternoon.

Hostile artillery more active in rear areas during hours of daylight. Gas projected into ST EMILE Sector at 1.20am.

Batteries fired at normal and slow rate until situation calmed down. Gas shelling appears to be on the increase.

Front very quiet during evening and first half of night.

The enemy is becoming increasingly aggressive. Plans are made for retaliatory shoots by both field and heavy artillery from well-prepared and strongly defended positions. Intelligence reports enemy activity will increase at 3 a.m. next morning.

BRAQUEMONT Feb/17. Cool. Frost at night. Visibility fair.

Hostile artillery active in rear areas. NOEUX LES MINES and HERSIN being shelled.

Details received of new line of DEFENCE called "ARMY LINE". Positions for defence of this line are called for at once. This line is well wired now.

Information received at 9pm that enemy has increased activity from 3am tomorrow morning.

Despite the increased enemy activity, information from prisoners seems to indicate that the Canadian Corps' front is not thought to be facing the main offensive. However, German troops are reported to be concentrating opposite the 1st Army in a nearby sector of the front. Manning artillery OPs continues to be a very dangerous occupation.

BRAQUEMONT Feb/18. Milder. Visibility poor in morning, fair in afternoon.

At 4.30am enemy laid down heavy barrage on our Front Line system north of NORMAN STACKS. SOS was called on CENTRE GROUP. One officer from wiring party is reported missing.

During the day enemy artillery quieter than usual on forward areas. Prisoner statements generally do not point to an offensive on this front. 5 German Divisions are reported in reserve opposite 1st Army Front, this indicating offensive action at some point near: present indications point to line between CAMBRAI and ARRAS.

Information obtained by our wireless was correct regarding enemy activity early this morning.

Above and below: An 18-pdr Mk IV on an Mk III carriage. (*Courtesy of the RCA Museum*)

Lieut. ARMSTRONG 7th Battery, wounded a week ago in an OP on HILL 70, died this morning at BARLIN.

BRAQUEMONT Feb/19. Mild. Visibility poor. Very misty in morning.

CRA visits proposed ANTI-TANK gun position north of LOOS.

Camouflage Officer Reports are received that six 18 pdrs have been received for ANTI-TANK purposes of which 1st Can. Division get three.

Enemy very active with gas on ST EMILE Section and on LOOS during early morning.

Artillery memorial at LES TILLEULS corner VIMY RIDGE was unveiled by Gen CURRIE at 3pm in presence of Gen. HORNE and Gen. BYNG and representatives of all artillery units in Canadian Corps.

Plans are made for much heavier retaliation when intelligence indicates where concentrations of enemy artillery and infantry mass in preparation for attacks. The heavy Newton 6-inch trench mortars are beginning to be effective in use.

BRAQUEMONT Feb/20. Cool & windy with light rain in the afternoon.

6" Newtons are beginning to find favor with infantry. They were used with effect during early morning against active machine guns on HILL 70 Section.

Front generally very quiet.

New scheme for Heavy Retaliation issued – all guns howitzers, TMs in the Division fire One, Two or Three Rounds Gun Fire on specific points or areas. Zero Time is given by firing Triple Green parachute rocket from CENTRE GROUP Hdqrs.

Artillery positions for Defence of Army Line between HERSIN and HOUCHIN are reconnoitered.

Demand for more ammunition has been sent to Division. Present supply does not meet the demands for opportunity targets and harassing fire, not taking into account the firing to be done at request of infantry for retaliation and protection.

Increased movement behind enemy lines engages the interest and action of field artillery. OPs are once again being detected and harassed by enemy shell fire.

BRAQUEMONT Feb/21. Fair and mild. Visibility very good in morning and fair in afternoon.

Movement above normal in rear areas. Many Targets taken on by 18 pdrs.

CRA attends conference of Senior General Officers at Corps Hdqrs to confer on general situation at present.

Front fairly normal during day and at night. Battery areas slightly shelled. One of our RIGHT GROUP OPs destroyed by shell fire.

German tanks are increasingly regarded as a serious threat and anti-tank weapons are being carefully positioned to deal with them effectively.

BRAQUEMONT Feb/22. Dull with light rain. Very windy. Visibility poor. Front quiet.

Special Tank Gun positions are detailed by "G" Can. Corp. Policy is to keep guns for dealing with tanks at least 1500 yards from Front Line. Guns will be placed north of LOOS, on LOOS Crassier and on table land north of FOSSE 12.

Individual movement considerable in back areas.

BRAQUEMONT Feb/23. Mild. Visibility very poor.

Front normally quiet. Slight shelling of battery areas near LOOS.

CRA visits ANTI-TANK positions and details work to be proceeded with at once but everything to be done under camouflage.

Trench Mortar ammunition situation is improving. In the meantime Heavy Artillery have special allotment to deal with TM emplacements.

Another large-scale raid is being proposed to overrun an enemy headquarters post that has been detected.

BRAQUEMONT Feb/24. Dull with rain at intervals. Visibility poor.

Proposed to make a raid to cover one of the enemy Battn. Hdqrs on HILL 70 Section.

Estimated that over 50,000 rounds 18 pounder ammunition will be needed.

Front normally quiet. A large amount of more or less disguised registration took place on LOOS and FOSSE 14 Areas.

BRAQUEMONT Feb/25. Dull with rain. Very windy. Visibility very fair.

Corps Camouflage Officer visits the 3 Special ANTI-TANK gun locations with Brigade Commanders and arranges necessary details for camouflaging.

Front very quiet in view of the good visibility. Nothing more than the usual scattered shelling of LOOS area.

Artillery duels are the order of the day, with the enemy firing on unoccupied positions. Their intelligence is clearly giving them out-of-date information.

However, weather conditions are not good enough for the Canadians to achieve the success they had hoped for.

BRAQUEMONT Feb/26. Mild and slightly misty. Very windy. Visibility poor.

JOYRIDE shoot on BOIS de Quatorze at 7.15am at request of Left Infantry Brigade. Owing to mist the Triple Green Rocket was hard to see: result being that shoot was ragged.

Enemy shelled several unoccupied battery positions thru the day with 10.5 and 15cm. One of these positions is an alternative position on which work has been done in the past week. Front quiet.

Except for shooting on empty positions practically no hostile activity in back areas.

Rumours of the anticipated enemy offensive continue to arrive. This time they suggest that the front to the north is to be attacked.

BRAQUEMONT Feb/27. Dull & windy. Visibility poor owing to mist.

Heavy bombardment at 3am towards HULLUCH during enemy raid.

Message received that prisoner captured this morning gives 28th as beginning of enemy offensive – starting point high ground north of GEHLUVELT in BELGIUM.

Front fairly quiet. 6th Battery Forward Gun shelled very heavily. 9.45am TM in ST MILE Section heavily shelled on opening fire.

BRAQUEMONT Feb/28. Fair with showers of snow. Visibility fair.

Commander-in-Chief visit 1st Can. Div. in afternoon and meets CRA. 60th Battery Forward Gun shelled.

Front fair quiet.

Diaries for March 1918

The Canadian 1st Division's first month in the line had seen some enemy harassment and raiding, including more enemy counter battery work against artillery positions, but this was sporadic rather than continuous. Nevertheless, the troops in the line had to be vigilant, and the Canadians concentrated their resources on the areas where the long-awaited offensive was most likely to strike. Despite the fact that, in overall terms, Allied aircraft outnumbered German, enemy air activity had increased, making it difficult for the Allies to use observation balloons near the front.

The intelligence reports from all sources confirmed that the enemy build-up continued apace. There was little doubt that their offensive would begin within a matter of weeks, weather permitting, but it remained impossible for the Allies to forecast exactly where the first assaults were to strike. The greatest threat was in the enemy's potential to penetrate towards the coast, which would initially cut off the lateral rail connections serving the Allied forces. If this was achieved, then further advances towards the channel coast would be within Germany's grasp, eventually threatening shipping connections across the Channel to England. If successful, this would be a war-winning strategy.

The Allies were resigned to the fact that the enemy offensive would succeed in overwhelming their forces in places. However, the Canadian Corps, together with the other British forces to the north and south of their sector, had strongholds in the Vimy area, in the fortifications all over Vimy Ridge, and the adjoining areas around Hill 70 and the Scarpe River valley, which would prove difficult for the enemy to overcome. If they could be held, they would provide vital means of attacking the enemy flanks and communications from carefully planned artillery positions, which were rapidly being completed.

The general Allied policy, using the strategic position of the Canadian Corps, was to develop their defences and to make life behind the advancing German front line as difficult as possible. If successful, this would delay or even deter assaults in their area. The planning and execution of these deterrents were the main activities of the Canadian Corps in the first weeks of March.

BRAQUEMONT Mar/1. Mild. Slightly misty. Visibility fair. Flurries of rain and sleet.

CRA visits ELVASTON CASTLE (Left Group Hdqrs) to confer on proposed raid of Can. Inf. Bde.

Front fairly quiet. OPs on HILL 70 heavily shelled at intervals.

BRAQUEMONT Mar/2. Very cool with high wind. Snow during morning. Visibility good during morning, poor in the afternoon.

Very heavy Drum Fire heard towards north from 5.45am to 5.30am. Large raid on Portugese.

New OPs are being established in new areas which cover our whole Front Line Zone better than from established OPs on HILL 70.

CRA, Infantry Bde Commanders and DMGO held conference with GOC during afternoon. CRA 11th Division asks for cooperation in minor raid.

CRA 4th Can. Division asks to put guns for raid in old offensive positions in CITÉ JEANNE D'ARQ.

Hostile concentration of artillery and TMs near FOSSE 1 de LENS on our supports at 5.30pm lasting for 15 minutes.

BRAQUEMONT Mar/3. Cold and Damp. Snow still remains. Visibility poor.

Demonstration of Tanks with Infantry in the attack, during the morning at MARQUEFFLES FARM.

Concentrated shoot was placed on west edge of CITÉ St AUGUSTE at 7am. Infantry were quite satisfied with volume of fire in this case.

'PROTECT MASON' a call for barrage in the vicinity of MASON'S HOUSE was given by 3rd C.I. Bde at 10pm. Front fairly quiet with slight increase of hostile harassing fire in Forward Area.

BRAQUEMONT Mar/4. Dull and misty. Mist turned to light rain at intervals. Visibility poor.

Very heavy barrage on "ST EMILE" and "LENS" beginning at 5.45 am and continuing to 7.00am.

Enemy attempted to raid near ALOOF Trench. Barrage began on Front Line and supports, lifting partly to battery areas about 6.10am. All cross roads received attention.

MAJOR V KENT 55th Battery now with CENTRE GROUP was killed in the bombardment. Casualties fairly heavy in 16 Bn. Holding right subsection ST EMILE. None of our men are missing. Two prisoners taken by battalion of 2nd Can. Division on our right.

Front fairly quiet during the remainder of the day.

BRAQUEMONT Mar/5. Fairly cool. Fairly misty. Visibility fair at intervals.

Funeral of MAJOR KENT 5th CDA held at AIX NOULETTE Cemetery at 3.00pm attended by CRA.

5th Battery at FOSSE 7 de BETHUNE slightly shelled. Fairly quiet all day.

BRAQUEMONT Mar/6. Fine weather. Slight mist. Visibility good.

2nd Division raided on left portion of LENS Sector capturing one unwounded prisoner at 2.15am.

During the morning enemy harassed rear areas at intervals.

CRA visits Defensive Areas about LES BREBIS and BULLY GRENAY. Front fairly quiet.

BRAQUEMONT Mar/7. Fine and cool. Very misty in early morning. Visibility generally poor.

CRA visits positions about FOSSE 7 de BETHUNE with a view to placing 4 Howitzers of 48th Howitzer Battery in this area and having only one section in the Forward position behind LOOS Crassier.

Front quiet.

BRAQUEMONT Mar/8. Fine weather. Visibility very fair.

Gas was fired into Cite ST LAURENT and Cite ST PIERRE during early morning and at 7.30am concentration was put on forward position of ST PIERRE.

Arrangements made at 2nd Can. Inf. Bde. Hdqrs for several raids in near future. Raid by 33rd Inf. Bde. 11th Division proposed for early to-morrow morning.

Front fairly quiet. Sector on our left fairly lively.

BRAQUEMONT Mar/9. Fair and warm. Visibility fair at intervals.

33rd Inf. Bde. 11th Division on our immediate left raided enemy trenches at 4.45am but found no enemy. LEFT Group cooperated.

CRA visits special TANK Guns and finds everything satisfactory.

OC LEFT GROUP agrees that position at FOSSE 7 de BETHUNE selected by CRA is the best for Defensive warfare for 4 of the howitzers. Approval is being demanded from 1st Can. Division.

Word has been received from 1st Army that prisoner captured stated that a Feint attack would be made against the PORTUGESE at NEUVE CHAPELLE on early morning of 10th and that main attack would be on HILL 70. Prisoner's statement regarding DUMMY TANKS was verified from air photographs. Increased alertness was in force thru out the night. All harassing fire was cancelled and reserved for early morning concentration on TANK Assembly areas.

Summer Time comes into effect at 11pm – 11pm becoming midnight.

BRAQUEMONT Mar/10. Fine weather. Slight mist. Visibility good at times.

Nothing resulted in early morning excepted distant drum fire for an hour towards north which was raid near NEUVE CHAPELLE.

TANK Shooting demonstration by picked teams from 7 DAs at ZOOAVE VALLEY south of SOUCHEZ resulted in 7th Battery (1st CDA) shooting 7th in the competition and with its 7th Round destroying the TANK completely.

Arrangements completed by Four raids by 2nd Can. Div. Bde. On HILL 70 Section. Trench Mortars are cutting wire and 18 pdrs sweeping it up. Front fairly quiet.

BRAQUEMONT Mar/11. Fine. Very misty in early morning.

Wire cutting for the raids is progressing very favorably. Slight "mix-up" in actual location of gaps cut by TMs which were pointed out by Infantry officers. This was straightened out later.

CENTRE GROUP are arranging direct with 8th Battn. Regarding raid "D" directly north of NORMAN STACKS Area. This will probably take place on morning of 13th.

BRAQUEMONT Mar/12. Fine weather continues. Heavy ground mist in early morning.

Enemy aeroplane drove down our balloons between NOEUX-LES-MINES and BETHUNE. GOTHA landed near HERSIN during the night and was burned by the crew. 2 Officers & 2 NCOs were captured.

Gaps for raids "A" & "B" were reported OK by Infantry. All arrangements completed for the raid. Zero Hour is set at 9pm. Enemy retaliation opened at 9.03 on our right supports. Heavy retaliation reported during cutting of wire of false gaps near NORMAN STACKS.

Captures during raid are 2 ORs and 1 m.g. Enemy appear to clear all positions which may be raided as soon as our barrage falls. Infantry casualties very slight.

BRAQUEMONT Mar/13. Very fine. Slight Haze. Visibility very fair at intervals.

Enemy artillery is more active on HILL 70 area due no doubt to our activity of last night. 9.2 Howitzer Battery near PHILOSOPHE is being shelled daily with heavy calibre. Several dumps have been blown up in this locality recently.

Hauling a 9.2-inch Howitzer into position through a ruined town. (*Courtesy of the RCA Museum*)

Prospective raids "C"&"D" by 2nd Can. Inf. Bde. Will not take place at present.

First orders received regarding a very large gas projection to take place 15/16.

BRAQUEMONT Mar/14. Rain in early morning clearing towards noon.

Artillery covering ST EMILE Section passes to 4th Can. Division at 10am. 1st CDA retains two 18 pdr batteries of 5th CDA (being relieved by 2nd CDA) for support of the HILL 70 Sector.

Front fairly quiet.

BRAQUEMONT Mar/15. Fine and cool. Slight haze. Visibility fair at intervals.

Details of gas projection received from Division and Corps. Zero Hour was set for 11pm but unfavorable wind resulted in postponement.

GOC 1st Can. Div. with CRA visited 1st CDAC to inspect during afternoon. Quite successful. GOC arranged for Div. band which during afternoon at HOUCHIN.

Brig. Gen. THACKER temporarily commands 1st Can. Div. in absence of GOC who proceeded on English leave.

BRAQUEMONT Mar/16. Fine weather. Visibility fair in afternoon.

Front fair quiet all day till 7.52 pm when heavy concentration opened on ST EMILE Section. Right GROUP fired SOS for 5 minutes then turning to HELP NORMAN. Enemy raiders repulsed leaving two unwounded and one wounded prisoner in hands of brigade covering ST EMILE.

Gas projection again postponed.

BRAQUEMONT Mar/17. Fair weather. Visibility good.

Front slightly active. Enemy increased his activity against Trenches on HILL 70. 6th Battery Forward Gun Position (temporarily vacated) heavily shelled with 4.1s thru out the morning.

Slight increase in enemy aerial activity. Low flying plane engaged by many artillery LEWIS Guns with good results.

Increased enemy movement, new work – trench railway etc seen behind BOIS DE QUATORZE.

Gas projection again postponed.

BRAQUEMONT Mar/18. Fine weather continues.

CRA visits 1st and 3rd Battery positions and RIGHT Group OPs.

A few further arrangements are being made for raids by 4th Can. Division and 11th Division on our flanks. Intention is that Right Group cooperates with 4th Can. Div. creating a diversion by artillery bombardment on Cite ST AUGUSTE: LEFT Group will produce Smoke Screen and cooperate in barrage.

Usual scattered shelling on HILL 70. Front fairly quiet.

Word was received that gas projection would be made but at 11pm owing to tricky winds it was postponed.

BRAQUEMONT Mar/19. Dull with rain. Visibility poor.

Quiet day. Usual light shelling of supports.

Enemy laid down practice Smoke screen on our left in evening.

BRAQUEMONT Mar/20. Dull with rain. Cleared to better weather at noon.

Gas projection postponed owing to Bde relief on HILL 70 Sector.

Quiet Day.

It would be the last quiet day that the Canadian Corps would experience for some considerable time.

CHAPTER TWO

Providing Rapid Response to German Threats on a Wide Front

21 March – 25 May 1917

When the long-awaited German campaign opened on 21 March, their main concentration was against the southern part of their front, seeking to bypass Vimy Ridge and turn the flank beyond it to cut off the salient they hoped to create. The divisions of the Canadian Corps, in the absence of General Currie who was attending a conference in England, were separately deployed to defend the areas under immediate threat. When General Currie returned to his headquarters in France, he found that he remained in direct command of the 3rd and 4th Divisions of the Canadian Corps. The 1st Division went into the Army Reserve in the Chateau de la Haie area and the 2nd Division went into General Headquarters Reserve in the Mont St Eloi area. Both 1st and 2nd Divisions were then placed under orders of the 3rd British Army. The 4th Division was relieved at the front and went into General Headquarters Reserve. Subsequently, command of the 3rd Division came under orders of the XIII Corps. Thus pressure of circumstances, following the German attacks, had brought the four divisions of the Canadian Corps under orders of the 3rd and 4th British Armies.

It was a time when response to developing enemy attacks was all-important and the Canadian divisions were frequently moved to provide reinforcements wherever they were most needed. Sometimes while in transit to another part of the front, orders would change again. At the end of March, the 1st and 2nd Canadian Divisions were deployed under orders with the 3rd Army and the 3rd and 4th Divisions with the 1st Army. The divisions with the 1st Army came under the command of General Currie once again.

On 9 April the Germans opened a second major attack to the north, leaving the Canadians in a deep salient to counter part of this new threat.

Thus the 1st, 3rd and 4th Divisions, now under General Currie, held a rather thinly stretched front of 29,000 yards. In order to deceive the enemy, these divisions adopted a very aggressive attitude. Artillery constantly harassed the enemy's forward and rear areas and infantry penetrated the enemy lines with fighting patrols and raiding parties. Everywhere along this part of the front all possible means were employed to discourage the Germans, who had made considerable penetrations of the British lines to the north. Through continuously attacking their flanks, the Canadians made the enemy reconsider advancing further on this front. From 10 April to 7 May, when they were finally relieved, the 1st, 3rd and 4th Canadian Divisions held their front of 29,000 yards and the 2nd Division, then with the VI Corps, held one of 6,000 yards.

Having been relieved on 7 May, the 1st, 3rd and 4th Divisions went into General Headquarters Reserve in the 1st Army area – all except the field artillery of the 1st Canadian Division, which remained in active operations against the enemy, as is shown in the diary entries. The 2nd Division, meanwhile, remained in the line with the 3rd Army.

On 25 May, the 1st Canadian Divisional Artillery HQ moved to Berles where most of the Canadian Corps were to concentrate in training areas.

------ooo------

Diaries for 21 March 1918 Onwards

On 19 March General Currie had been asked to attend a conference in London; he returned on a torpedo boat destroyer conveying other senior officers who had been on leave in England and arrived back at his Corps Headquarters at 8 p.m. on 22 March. On his return he found that his 1st and 2nd Canadian Divisions, which had been in reserve to relieve his 3rd and 4th Divisions in the line, had already been transferred to Army and GHQ Reserves respectively. This temporarily broke up the Canadian Corps, leaving him in command of only half of it. He was unhappy with this arrangement.

The first days of the German assaults from 21 March onwards involved the 1st CDA in their reserve role in support of the divisions in the line.

BRAQUEMONT Mar/21. Fine weather, slightly misty.

Enemy laid down intense bombardment of supports and Front Line on HILL 70. Sector from 5.40 to 6.15 am.

A raid was made on LEFT Battalion at 5.45am with heavy casualties to enemy.

Requests from South indicate enemy has begun his offensive on a fifty mile front from BULLECOURT to LA FERE. Gas projection was carried off at 11pm quite successfully. Retaliation heavy on 1st Corps to left.

The 1st CDA clearly had a significant active role at this stage but the 2nd CDA, in GHQ Reserve rather than under the command of the Canadian Corps, was already about to be transferred. Furthermore, the 5th CDA (the only element of the 5th Canadian Division to be deployed) was to take over from the 1st CDA which itself was being transferred to Army Reserve.

At this time the Brigade Major of 5th CDA was Major H. D. G. Crerer. Crerer would play a very important part in the work of the CBSO when McNaughton moved on to take up the post of Commander of Canadian Heavy Artillery in place of Brigadier General R. H. Massie who retired due to ill health.

BRAQUEMONT Mar/22. Fine weather continues for enemy offensive.

Enemy has apparently not got the success he ought to have had from the number of divisions employed.

Heavy bombardment of rear areas to our left from 12 midnight to 1am. Nothing further received from South.

Our front fairly quiet. HILL 70 Sector is covered by 1st CDA batteries alone from 7pm, 2nd CDA batteries rejoining 2nd Can. Div. which takes over a sector near the SCARPE.

4th Can. Div. relieve HILL 70 Sector on 23rd. 5th CDA relieve 1st CDA on 23rd.

BRAQUEMONT Mar/23. Fine weather continues. No important news from the South.

NOEUX-LES-MINES shelled and bombed during the night. 5th CDA carry out relief of batteries during afternoon.

Slight discussion over the handing over of "Illuminating Sight Sets". Front remains normally quiet.

Already the new arrangement – the splitting up of the Canadian Corps – seems to be causing some confusion. However, 1st CDA is now employed in the preparation of secondary lines of defence in order to be able to provide defence in depth in the event of a breakthrough by the enemy.

BRAQUEMONT & CHATEAU DE LA HAIE Mar/24. Fine and very misty in morning clearing in afternoon.

Slight bombardment both north and south of HILL 70 between 4 and 6am when enemy attempted raid on 3rd Can. Division south of SOUCHEZ.

Command of artillery covering HILL 70 passes to CRA 4th Can. Division at 10am and not to GOC 5th Can. Div. Artillery as was intended. This change occurred owing to 4th Can. Div. assuming command at 10am of HILL 70 Sector.

1st Can. Div. Arty. Hdqrs move to CHATEAU DE LA HAIE in morning. Reconnaissance of new positions for MAISON BLANCH – BAILLEUL Line, which were dug during last night, is made by CRA. Visited also the area between ROCLINCOURT and Heights immediately north of SCARPE in vicinity of LE POINT DU JOUR Redoubt.

General impression seems to be that enemy offensive between the SCARPE and LA FERE is well in hand. Intelligence gleaned from prisoners suggests a minor offensive near or south of LA BASSÉE.

1st Bde CFA is ordered to go into action in RED LINE positions about midnight.

CHATEAU DE LA HAIE Mar/25. Dull with cold wind. Visibility poor.

Heavy bombardment heard from 1st [Army] Corps front to our left – later reported 1st [Army] Corps captured 13 prisoners during early morning.

1st Bde are in action before daybreak and are under tactical orders of 4th Can. Div. Artillery.

1st Can. Div. Trench Mortar brigade is attached to 4th Can. Div. Arty. from 10am.

Trouble seems to be expected on the left.

4th Division Batteries have orders to be prepared to run out of pits and swing left.

All Divisional Artilleries are now under Tactical Orders of GOCRA Canadian Corps. This is in accordance with policy laid down in Can. Corps. Defence Scheme viz. GOCRA assumes tactical command of all artillery when extensive operations are contemplated.

'STAND TO' received at 11pm to move at One Hours notice from 5.30am tomorrow. This is probably due to statement from prisoner captured.

CHATEAU DE LA HAIE Mar/26. Fair and cool.

Counter measures carried out from 4am to 6am on enemy system south of ACHEVILLE where prisoner stated attack was to be made this morning at daybreak.

Latest contemplated move is to take over the line from 11th and part of 46th Division between present north Corp Boundary and LA BASSÉE Canal. This move was cancelled at 5.30pm and the whole Corps will probably go south.

Units of 1st Can. Div Arty. are to move into Reserve area tomorrow.

CHATEAU DE LA HAIE Mar/27. Dull and cool.

Units march at times from 6.00 to 7.30am – 1st Bde to ACQ; 2nd Bde to FREVIN CAPELLE; 1st CDAC and 1st Cdn. T M Bde to GOUY SERVINS. All destinations reached by 10.00am. 1st Cdn. TM Bde is attached to 1st CDAC from 10.00am until further order.

Cdn. Corps is being relieved at noon today by 1st and 13th [Army] Corps – Inter Corps boundary SOUCHEZ RIVER.

4th Cdn. Div. is being relieved by 10.00am 29th when Cdn. Corps HQ; 1st and 4th Divisions will be in Army Reserve. After 29th [April] 5th CDA becomes GHQ Reserve.

At this stage, General Currie had only the 4th Canadian Division under his direct command, having handed over command of the 3rd Canadian Division to GOC XIII Corps the previous night. 1st CDA remained in reserve.

CHATEAU DE LA HAIE/ETRUN Mar/28. Cool and windy. Rain in afternoon.

Infantry began moving about 2am.

Artillery Units moved between 7.30 & 8.30am.

On road between HAUTEVILLE and COUTURELLE Orders received to proceed back to LARESSET – MONTENESCOURT Area.

Two brigades arrived "Y" Hutments and DAC at MONTENESCOURT at dusk. Mens quarters fair. Headquarter in house at ETRUN evacuated by ANTI AIRCRAFT Section.

Instructions were received at 17th Corps during the evening to put the two brigades into action South of ARRAS on the morning of 29th.

Sudden change in destination was due to heavy enemy attack between OPPY and GOMMECOURT.

Another change in reporting and command arrangements for 1st CDA is implemented. They are formally part of the wider command under the British 3rd Army rather than the Canadian Corps.

ETRUN/CITADEL ARRAS Mar/29. Dull and cool. Rain at intervals.

Brigades leave wagon lines at 5.00am.

Guns go into action in the open. All batteries get into action without mishap. Practically no enemy shelling.

1st CDA forms a sub Group temporarily under CRA 15th [British] Div. Arty. Orders received that 1st Cdn. Div. take over 1 Bde Front and will be covered by 1st Cdn. Div. Arty. Relief will probably be completed about daylight tomorrow.

13-pdr anti-aircraft guns mounted on a lorry. (*Courtesy of the RCA Museum*)

Front of 1st Cdn. Div. is about 1000 (yds) in length with a strong Switch Line along South Div. Boundary. 2nd Cdn. Div. are on our right.

ARRAS (CITADEL) Mar/30. No enemy attack developed at daybreak. Quiet during night.

Spasmodic shelling of our front from 7.00am – 9.00am. All 1st CDA Guns put on Area shoot at 9.15am on tender points.

Enemy begin shelling huge engineering dump and 2nd Brigade positions close by. A few casualties resulted – one gun fit for IOM [scrap].

ARRAS (CITADEL) Mar/31. Fine and cool.

Quarters in Citadel are very cramped and damp.

After good air reconnaissance enemy shelled the Citadel intermittently during morning and early afternoon. Fire was probably directed against ANTI AIRCRAFT Section in rear.

Much back areas strafing with HV [High Velocity German] Guns during the day.

Several area shoots put on 2nd Bde Batteries. CRA decides to move them to new positions tonight.

Heavy Artillery Brigades consisting of 2– 60 pdr Batteries and 2– 6" Howitzer Batteries placed at disposal of CRA 1st Cdn. Div.

Artillery situation is very good on 17th Corps in so far as number of guns both heavy and light is concerned.

1st Cdn. Div. takes over 300 yards more front to north from 15th Division.

Reports today give better news from the South. MONDIDIER is again in hands of the French.

Diaries for April 1918

ARRAS – WARLUS Apr/1. Fine weather.

Headquarters move from CITADEL ARRAS to huts in WARLUS where "G" Staff 1st Cdn. Division is established. Accommodation is however very poor.

CRA visits batteries during morning. 5th and 6th Batteries have moved position during night.

Positions vacated were strafed heavily during the day much to the enjoyment of 2nd Bde gunners. Harassing fire is increased during night.

Enemy appears to be quite disturbed with the increased volume of fire during hours of darkness.

WARLUS Apr/2. Fine weather.

Enemy is very active during early morning on forward slope of TELEGRAPH HILL. Fire appears to come from 77 [mm] batteries in front of MONCHY-LES-PREUX. Several area shoots were carried out and nothing more was heard from these.

Activity increased to such an extent that COUNTER PREPARATION was given at 6.30 am.

Later day was quiet except for the usual Back Area harassing fire.

Enemy gas-shelled BEURAINS and back slopes of TELEGRAPH HILL about 8pm in spite of drizzling rain.

WARLUS Apr/3. Dull and cool.

Very quiet night and morning.

Notice received that Front will be extended 700 yds to north making a total of 2000 yds for Div. Front.

SOS lines change to cover new front at 7pm and Div. take over at 5am tomorrow morning.

WARLUS Apr/4. Dull with rain. Visibility poor all day.

Considerable sniping during the day of area between BEURAINS and TELEGRAPH HILL.

Enemy doesn't appear to be making much effort to dig in and consolidate. His idea apparently is to prepare for another attack in direction of ARRAS.

No news from South except that everything is fairly stationary.

WARLUS Apr/5. Rain. Visibility poor.

Heavy barrage along the front from the SCARPE to beyond 2nd Cdn. Division to our right about 7am. Enemy attempted to raid.

COUNTER PREPARATION at 9am quietened the situation.

Heavy firing during the course of the morning when 34th Division to the right made a raid supported by Tanks.

48th Battery and 4th Battery positions are becoming more and more harassed by enemy fire. New positions are being reconnoitered for these batteries.

1st CDA is being retained to support other non-Canadian formations in the British 1st Army while the rest of its own division's formations are to be relieved.

WARLUS Apr/6. Changeable weather. Fine in the morning turning to dull and cool in evening. Front fairly quiet.

New action laid down for all 18 pdrs, 4.5 Hows [Howitzers] and 6" Hows when answering SOS Signal. After 3 minutes intense fire on normal SOS lines the barrages of above mentioned guns & how's move forward 100 yds every two minutes for ten minutes and then come back to normal barrage lines. This action can be repeated at any stage thru out SOS on code word "COMB" being given.

Division less Artillery will be relieved before 8th inst. by 56th [British] Division. Enemy is being harassed to a very considerable extent nightly which must hamper his preparations for further offensive. 1200– 18 pdrs [Field Guns], 600– 4.5 How[Howitzer], 200– 6" How, 250– 60 pdrs is being fired during hours of darkness on new work, battery positions, roads & approaches.

WARLUS Apr/7. Fair in morning with rain in afternoon.

Quiet night with exception of usual enemy artillery flurry on our trenches between 6 and 7am.

SOS Signal changes at noon from Red to Green Very Lights. These Very Lights will not prove satisfactory. This was exemplified yesterday when a ground mist obscured six signals sent up from our outpost line near BOIS de BOEUFS.

CRA gets information at 17th Corps DUISANS that 56th Div. Arty. will relieve our brigades on 8th inst.

A battery of 60-pounders in action late in the war. Two Canadian Heavy Batteries in the Canadian Corps Heavy Artillery were equipped with these guns. (*F. Wade Moses, Montreal, courtesy of the RCA Museum*)

CRA 56th Division arrives to look over the general situation. Agreement made that he will take over command as soon as relief is completed.

1st CDA Hdqrs move to BERLES tomorrow.

Move of 4th Battery Section cancelled.

Gun dumps increased to 600x18 pdr per gun and 400x4.5 per Howitzer. This increase in dumps is due to our being taken over by 1st ARMY.

Southern Army Boundary is our present Southern Boundary.

WARLUS – ST AUBANS Apr/8. Dull with rain at intervals.

Relief by 56th Div. Artillery is completed during hours of daylight. Wagon lines and DAC of 56th Div. Arty. arrive at 1st CDA wagon lines about noon.

Personnel of 1st CDA Battery positions relieved by 3.00pm. 1st CDA march to ANZIN area during the afternoon.

Headquarters 1st CDA are situated in RED CHATEAU, ST AUBANS.

The next move is to a sector where 1st CDA is mainly concerned with defensive preparations to deter enemy penetration. 9 April marks the opening of the second major assault by the Germans. This time it is to the north of the part of the front where the Canadians are mainly operating. Map 2 shows the disposition of the divisions of the Canadian Corps on 8 April.

ST AUBANS – ETRUN Apr/9. Fair weather.

1st CDA relieve 4th Div. Artillery on front between BROKEN MILL east of OBSERVATION RIDGE south of SCARPE to point SW of GAVRELLE.

About 1500 yds along southern Divisional Front is swampy terrain. Divisional Front is not covered by continuous 18 pdr barrage owing to limited 18 pdr strength.

Barrage is placed across valleys and in areas thru which enemy would probably attack.

Relief of 4th DA is carried out during daylight and is complete by 3pm. Communication is very poor owing probably to use of air lines [wires on poles frequently damaged by enemy fire and carelessness] up to recent date throughout area between Batteries and the rear country.

Word received that 2nd Div. Artillery now in ACQ area will reinforce 1st Cdn. Div. Front – one brigade will move into positions tomorrow. Front remains fairly quiet.

Enemy harassing fire over rear areas increased owing possibly to "enemy drive" in GIVENCHY – FLEURBAIX Area.

ETRUN Apr/10. Fair weather.

41st [British] Brigade RFA move into position. Bde & Battery Commanders arrive at 9.30am to go forward and reconnoiter positions. All positions are open.

Headquarters evacuated by 3rd Can. Inf. Bde. Hdqrs in RAILWAY TRIANGLE will be HDQRS 41st Bde RFA. 17th Bty.

41st Bde RFA relieves 1st Battery CFA in position south of SCARPE in the area in which 41st Bde batteries will go into action.

1st Battery CFA moves to position in BLANGY Park. Ammunition expenditure is increased to at least 3500 rds 18 pdr and 1500 rds 4.5 How. [Howitzer] per day. Gun dumps are increased 800 rds 18 pdr [Field Gun] and 600 rds 4.5 How.

Enemy is using gas concentrations against batteries. As practically no gas proof shelters exist several gas cases are reported both to officers and men.

Orders are issued that will facilitate the coordination of fire on areas to be nominated by infantry liaison officers for retaliatory shoots. This will enable heavy concentrations of fire to be brought to bear by guns within range of the sector(s) identified. This is a further example showing the value of the work of the CBSO in enabling the concerted fire power of all divisional field artillery units within range, as well as the Corps heavy artillery, to be brought to bear on a particular target area.

ETRUN Apr/11. Fair weather. Visibility poor.

Batteries in new positions register satisfactorily.

Word received that Divisional front will be extended northwards during the night 11/12th to BAILLEUL POST an addition of 1300 yds.

36th [British] Bde RFA on completion of extension of front will be transferred in present position to 1st Can. Div. Arty. This completes the 2nd DA with 1st Can. Div. Arty.

2nd DA Hdqrs. will be established at ETRUN on 12th.

Canadian Corps on completion of all reliefs now in progress will extend from immediately south of SCARPE to CHALK PIT ALLEY north of HILL 70.

Front remains quite normal.

ETRUN Apr/12. Fine weather. Visibility very good.

Artillery covering Front is divided into 4 Groups – two to each infantry brigade.

Owing to swampy nature of ground along SCARPE, the artillery disposition is as follows: GROUPS 1 & 2 covering Right Infantry Bde. 5– 18pdr batteries and 2– 4.5 Howitzer Batteries. GROUPS 3 & 4 covering Left Inf Bde. 7– 18 pdr and 2– 4.5 Howitzer Batteries.

Very quiet day on 1st Cdn. Div. Front.

Arrangements are proposed for new grouping of the Div'l Artillery with a view to placing of the two brigades of 2nd Divisional Artillery on one flank.

ETRUN Apr/13. Dull. Visibility poor.

Inter group relief between Groups 2 & 4 takes place. This places 41st and 36th Bdes RFA on the right covering Right Inf. Bde. These two brigades from 6pm operate as one group with 2nd DA Hdqrs as Group Headquarters. Front quiet.

ETRUN Apr/14. Dull and windy.

CRA visits 1st Brigade in its new positions near ROCLINCOURT and also 2nd Bde CFA.

Instruction in some old F.A.T. [Field Artillery Tactics] principle[s] will be given by both Brigades – to produce even better results against the Hun than we might do.

Decrease in enemy shell fire and great increase in movement. Several hostile batteries gallop into action north of FRESNES LES MONTAUBAN. Whether the Hun is trying to camouflage his actions by these Fool Tactics is not known as yet. Hostile batteries mentioned above were immediately heavily shelled by our Counter Batteries.

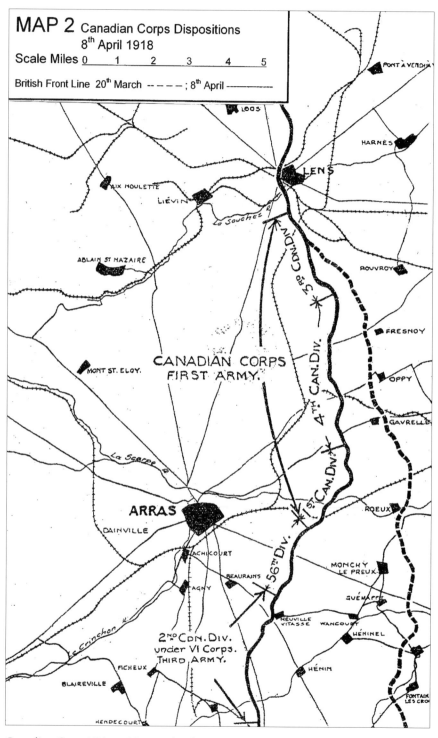

Canadian Corps' Dispositions, 8 April 1918.

Owing to abnormal movement "G" Staff wish to put on Counter Preparation in the morning. This will not be called for unless urgently needed as the extent of our SOS barrage lines would be divulged.

Enemy artillery remains calm thru out the night.

Preparations are to be made to facilitate the movement of artillery pieces and ammunition to new defensive positions by the construction of cross-country tracks. These will enable better support and defence in depth should the enemy break through.

ETRUN Apr/15. Dull and windy. Very cool weather. Visibility fair at intervals.

Night and early morning passed quietly.

Heavy artillery carried out double harassing fire thru out the hours of darkness. Field Artillery carried out heavy harassing fire from 4am – 6.30am. One Heavy Bde of 1st Cdn Div Heavy Group left for north this morning. This weakens heavy artillery on 1st Cdn Div Front slightly.

Artillery Cross-Country Tracks are being made passable for wagons and guns. This began with track from present battery positions to rear defensive

9.2-inch Howitzers being towed by a tractor. (*Courtesy of the RCA Museum*)

positions with the idea of avoiding shelled roads and corners. This idea has now extended to the point where horse transport will use cross country tracks in Rear Areas thereby leaving roads free for Tractor Guns etc etc.

Abnormal movement again is reported during the late afternoon.

ETRUN Apr/16. Dull with signs of rain.

Double harassing fire during early morning darkness again was ordered due to the fact that enemy could not, it was thought, have carried out any relief on the night 14/15th.

Front remains very quiet. Our policy is to force the enemy to relieve or reinforce the Divisions opposing us by inflicting casualties on him. Heavy harassing fire is carried out through out the night and misty days on all areas of activity and approaches.

Four reinforcement officers arrive of which three are "Old Timers"; Capt STEACY, Capt HAYES and Capt TAYLOR.

ETRUN – CHATEAU D'ACQ Apr/17. Dull with high wind.

CRA visits forward area – POINT DU JOUR locality.

1st Cdn Div Hdqrs move to CHATEAU D'ACQ. It was thought that if an attack were launched by enemy this locality in ETRUN would be out of communication almost at once due to HV [High Velocity German] shelling.

Front remains fairly quiet. New policy adopted – Roving guns will use up ammunition at various old positions about the forward area. This will give good instruction in ranging etc to new subalterns and in fact all battery officers.

Ammunition is now on allotment. It is more or less elastic however.

CHATEAU D'ACQ Apr/18. Dull with wind and drizzling rain.

SOS line on Left Brigade Section (GAVRELLE) is brought in about 200 yards at places. This position of line is still being held by two platoons in dug-outs beyond Front line. Front fairly quiet.

CHATEAU D'ACQ Apr/19. Dull with rain and wind.

Activity to our right during early morning.

56th Division are pushing out their line. Enemy attempt to get this back during the evening but fail. Our Front very quiet.

Scattered shelling of back areas with Area Shoot on Forward Sections of 4th and 7th Batteries during late afternoon.

Enemy Batteries opposite northern corps front are given gas bombardment commencing 9.30pm.

Comprehensive orders are issued covering defensive policy for the movement of batteries in case of a breakthrough by the enemy. Particular attention is given to anti-tank defences in the employment of mobile forward guns. Furthermore, one flank gun from each 18-pdr battery is allocated to deal with deeper penetrations by tanks. It is emphasised also that SOS procedures in drawing attention to enemy attacks or concentrations of enemy troops are to take priority over all other signals. Procedures for the employment of trench mortars are set out for close infantry support. Detailed instructions regarding communications are given, with frequent tests to ensure that lines are open and effective.

CHATEAU D'ACQ Apr/20. Fair weather. Very cool. Visibility poor.

Hostile artillery slightly more active both on rear and forward areas. Heavy battery positions in BLANGY shelled during afternoon. Enemy intention seems more or less obscure at present on this front.

Hostile batteries engaged on routine fire are mostly far back – a few being sited forward.

Raid made during early morning by Right Battn Right Brigade. Identification secured.

15th Division during early morning pushed out patrols and advanced their line successfully.

Enemy attempted to counter attack at 10.20pm. SOS was sent up from Right Battn: activity however quickly passed to 15th Division Front.

About 10.40pm Right Group gave assistance to 15th Div. Arty. following which everything quietened.

CHATEAU D'ACQ Apr/21. Fair weather. Cool in morning and evening. Visibility fair all day.

Artillery cross-country tracks are now ready for use. These will eliminate all traffic thru ST CATHERINES, ROCLINCOURT and badly shelled Cross Roads.

Instead of dumping Ammunition at Reserve positions, one dump manned by DAC personnel is being made immediately S. of ROCLINCOURT in the valley and close to Light Railways. This is within 1000 yards of positions for defence of FEUCHY and TILLOY LINES.

MGRA [Major General Royal Artillery] First Army visits CRA this afternoon.

Enemy activity on all fronts is said to have quietened – possibly he was forced to come to this due to the disorganisation of many of his Divisions. It may however be a lull before a storm.

CHATEAU D'ACQ Apr/22. Fine and cool. Visibility fair.

CRA visits OPs in MISSOURI Trench during morning. Raiding will formulate our chief amusement during the next few days or weeks. No identification has been secured for considerable time on the front between the SCARPE and SOUCHEZ. 4th Cdn Div to our left failed to secure identifications during last night – several raids were attempted and heavy fighting took place.

Reconnaissance is being continued on the Switches for Defence of South end of Vimy Ridge.

Front remains fairly quiet although back areas are receiving considerable attention.

The enemy is frequently adopting the practice of evacuating infantry frontline positions as soon as a Canadian barrage indicates that there is to be a raid in the area. The Germans also keep their troops as far back as is practical, leaving a small number in the forward trenches.

CHATEAU D'ACQ Apr/23. Fine and warm.

Large raid carried out by 4th Battn. Immediately south of SCARPE supported by Right Group. Artillery barrages were classed excellent by infantry. No identifications secured owing to evacuation of raided portion by enemy.

Brig. Gen Thacker goes to Can. Corps for few days while GOC RA is absent. Lt Col Anderson becoming CRA 1st Cdn. Div. during this time. Heavy bombardment to our right beginning between 11pm and midnight and extending over a couple of hours.

Several large raids are contemplated in the immediate future by Left Inf. Bde. [3rd Can. Inf. Bde.]. Details are being worked out.

Orders are issued on 23 April on the use of Lewis and machine guns for anti-aircraft defences, including rules for the identification and engagement of hostile aircraft and airships by day and night.

CHATEAU D'ACQ Apr/24. Dull and cool.

Front remains extremely quiet.

Slight harassing fire by enemy.

Conference held at 3rd Can. Inf. Bde. Hdqrs. to discuss a raid to be made on night 26/27.

Everything appears favorable to excellent artillery support. Much Gunning began about 9.45pm south of SCARPE. This developed to such an extent that SOS was sent up by our infantry almost at our southern boundary. 15th Divisional Artillery fired at first on SOS on their own front and later gave assistance to our Right Battn. (4th C.I.Bn [Canadian Infantry Battalion]) Everything quietened about 11pm.

The 'SNOUT' being referred to is probably an enemy salient that is a priority target.

A 13-pdr firing from a trailer. (*Courtesy of the RCA Museum*)

CHATEAU D'ACQ Apr/25. Dull and misty. Fairly warm weather. Visibility poor all day.

Front is quiet during hours of daylight. Preparations are being made for the raid. It will be made opposite the "SNOUT" north of FAMPOUX by the 16th and 14th Battns. It is regrettable that it cannot be held in conjunction with raid being made by the 4th Cdn Division at ARLEUX.

Preparations for this latter include gassing of enemy's batteries with approximately 8000 rds by the Heavy Artillery. This should make quite a digression and would enable our infantry to make a greater success of a sudden thrust at the "SNOUT".

CHATEAU D'ACQ Apr/26. Dull and misty.

4th Cdn. Div. raid failed to secure an identification this morning which makes 3rd Bde raid all the more important. Raid is postponed again owing to the fact that new trench in NO MAN'S land is quite deep and habitable and will necessitate it being the 1st Objective. Barrage charts are altered.

Brig Gen Thacker returned from Cdn. Corps Hdqrs.

Enemy activity is light with not much night harassing fire.

CHATEAU D'ACQ Apr/27. Fair weather, misty.

Reserve lines (ECURIE, PILLAR, PADDOCK, STELOI and BOIS DES ALLEUX Switches) reconnoitered by Brigade Commanders. A few changes are made at the last moment for the raid. It may be very successful and on the other hand it may not, especially if the enemy have received any information from our actions that we propose raid on the "SNOUT" area. Front remains extremely quiet due possibly to misty weather. H.V. [High Velocity German] gun activity on our back areas has practically ceased.

CHATEAU D'ACQ Apr/28. Dull and misty. Very damp cool weather.

3rd Inf. Bde. Raid was very successful. Captures were at least 1 Off. 50 ORs and several machine guns and our casualties light. Infantry, Artillery and Wireless were branches represented amongst prisoners. Good information was given by artillery prisoner about batteries and trench mortars.

Rumor received during the evening that Can. Corps will be relieved almost at once. The destination is not known but everybody rather suspects a journey north to help out the "old 2nd Army" with whom the Canadians were for so long in 1915 and 1916.

Enemy artillery very active on whole area forward and rear opposite that raided this morning between 8.30 and 10.30 pm. Evidently the enemy artillery were in ignorance of our raid until it was over and this "area strafe" was the German "Come back" to please his infantry.

CHATEAU D'ACQ Apr/29. Dull and misty with slight squalls of rain.

Warning order received from 1st Division that Can Corps will be relieved commencing night 30/1st. No intimation as to where we go or what we do.

Later in the day rumors are received that a large enemy attack is in progress at KEMMEL and that in view of this the contemplated relief will be postponed.

Heavy harassing fire carried out during the afternoon – probably as a result of our successful raid. Enemy artillery apparently got no SOS call during our entire operation which fact no doubt brought forth investigations between enemy artillery and infantry staffs with the result that increased activity was ordered to make amends.

CHATEAU D'ACQ Apr/30. Rain.

Very quiet Day. Enemy held at all points yesterday consequently Corps relief proceeds.

3rd Can Division is being relieved by 24th and 20th Divisions – relief beginning tonight. 15th Divisional Artillery on our right are moving north to join their Division which is now in the BRUAY Area.

Later reports from the raid of the 28th April give a listening set and the Battalion Defence Scheme as captured. This latter furnishes very valuable information and will probably result in a Dummy Attack being put on to draw his reserves to assembly positions where our artillery can deal with them.

Orders are issued giving instructions to field artillery covering SOS lines with details of sweeping barrages. Also detailed are instructions for Newton Mortars showing fields of fire covering Canadian lines opposite the enemy front.

Diaries for May 1918

The German offensive had appeared to reach its apogee during April. However, in spite of these indications, the Allies could not relax their alertness. Some elements of the Canadian Artillery were to be maintained in a state of readiness to bombard any enemy positions that might be used to relaunch an assault in their sectors, and arrangements were in place to focus fire from all divisional artilleries within range on tender spots as identified by observers.

Field gun positions were constructed to enable guns to be taken out of their pits and turned in any direction required. This would allow fire to be brought to bear to threaten flanks of advancing enemy troops should they break through. Forward field gun positioning was made more flexible through the use of tanks to move them rapidly with their ammunition into new prepared positions as the need arose.

Trench mortars, especially the heavier 6-inch Newtons, were brought into forward areas so that their fire could be coordinated with that of the field artillery when responding to SOS calls from the infantry.

Canadian infantry was moved progressively into reserve areas in preparation for their training and tactical deployment in anticipation of the need for mobility in combating further German assaults. Artillery formations, however, were kept in great readiness to respond to SOS calls wherever they occurred within range. This was the first indication shown by British intelligence that the enemy offensive was likely to fail. Furthermore, preparations were being made to ensure that the Canadian Corps was ready to act as one of the attacking formations in an Allied offensive that could lead to an end to the war in 1918, rather than 1919 as had been assumed earlier.

The policy in May 1918 for 1st CDA was to assist in keeping up the pressure on the enemy in the Lens/Arras area while preparing for counter offensive operations elsewhere as and when the occasion for them arose.

CHATEAU D'ACQ May/1. Dull with rain at intervals.

Warning received in morning by R A Can Corps that 1st Can. Div. Arty. is to be relieved by 48th A F [Australian Field] Bde RFA on the nights of 2/3rd and 3/4th May. This is later confirmed by the Move Order.

As yet nothing regarding Inf. moves received by "G" 1st Can Div. In view of the fact that Canadians may probably be in action against Boche main offensive, the question of moving 6" Newtons forward is being seriously considered; 1st CDTM Bde Officers are busy experimenting with various two wheeled designs.

CHATEAU D'ACQ May/2. Fine weather but slightly misty.

48th AF Bde RFA arrives at ANZIN from near ALBERT. They will relieve 2nd Bde CFA tonight and tomorrow night. Apparently the 48th AF Bde has had a fairly strenuous time down south from gas shelling chiefly.

Slight activity on our forward sections during the afternoon.

Wire received late in the evening originating apparently at 1st Army Hdqrs to the effect that Field Artillery on this sector will not be reduced. This will necessitate 1st Bde CFA remaining in the line. Later information received makes it appear probable that sections of 48th AF Bde RFA will have to be recalled in the morning.

CHATEAU D'ACQ May/3. Fine weather. Slight mist. Visibility fair at times.

All moves and reliefs of 1st Can Div Arty are cancelled with the exception of 1st CDTM Bde which will be relieved by the 2nd DTM Bde. 48th AF Bde RFA is recalled to wagon lines at ANZIN – later to go to XVIII Corps holding the HILL 70 Area.

56th Division to our right is extending northwards tonight taking over from Southern Boundary to ARRAS/DOUAI Railway. This means a slight readjustment of SOS lines to take effect at 6am tomorrow morning.

HTM south of the SCARPE river is being handed over to 17th Corps. 2– 6" Newtons will be taken out as 56th Div Arty state they do not wish them in their present location in BATTERY Valley south of SCARPE.

CHATEAU D'ACQ May/4. Very fine weather. Visibility only fair.

Front is slightly active, more than usual probably due to good weather. Enemy harassed rear areas considerably.

11th Tank Battn visited by CRA and DTMO to arrange taking forward of 18 pdrs and 6" Newtons. It was considered that if a strong "Stone-boat" were built for ammunition it could be hauled along behind Tank and 18 pdr attached to rear. Suggestion was also made to have a bracket made behind Tank to which 18 pdr could be hooked – ammunition in this case could be carried on the Tank. Experiments will be tried in the next few days.

Rumor is passed about that enemy is going to attack between ALBERT to ARRAS on 5th. Increased alertness during the night and early tomorrow morning is ordered.

CHATEAU D'ACQ May/5. Rain. Visibility fair at intervals.

Much "Gunning" thru the early morning to the south. This is probably COUNTER PREPARATION being carried out on the 3rd Army Front.

1st CDTM Bde moved to HOUVIN-HOUVIGNEUL near FREVENT to undergo training.

Relief of 1st Canadian Division Infantry is being carried out. Relief of artillery not yet in sight. GOC insists that CRA proceed to Training Area with him. This will necessitate leaving our brigades in the line under 2nd Div Arty Hdqrs. Relief is expected very shortly and they will join the Division in the course of the next few days.

CHATEAU D'ACQ – HOUVIN May/6. Dull and cool.

Command of artillery covering FAMPOUX & ARLEUX Sections passed to CRA 2nd Division at 10am. At the same hour Hdqrs 1st Cdn Div Arty closed at CHATEAU D'ACQ and opened at HOUVIN. 1st Cdn Div, move to HERMAVILLE Area. Quarters at HOUVIN are very fair although there is much crowding which will be worse when 1st CDAC arrive.

Arrangements are being made to put some troops under canvas.

HOUVIN May/7. Rain clearing toward noon.

CRA makes reconnaissance of area about HINGES (near BETHUNE). OPs in this area are very few. Due to the flatness of the ground and the innumberable buildings and trees it is almost impossible to get even a meagre view from any one OP. Tower in HINGES Chateau grounds gives a good view north of LUCON.

HOUVIN May/8. Fine weather.

Heavy firing thru out the night and early morning: later reported to have been Counter Preparation carried out at various places on the 3rd Army Front between ARRAS and ALBERT.

CRA attended conference at HOUDAIN – presumed to be regarding "DELTA" (large contemplated operation by the Canadian Corps) but found to be advance orders to proceed back to ARRAS to take command of our two artillery brigades which are still in the line. Information has apparently been obtained from prisoners that enemy intend to make an attack on the night of 9/10th May.

Rumours of enemy preparations to attack along the Canadian Corps' front continue to be received and the state of alertness is well justified.

HOUVIN – MAROEOIL May/9. Fine weather continues. Roads very dusty.

Artillery Hdqrs move from HOUVIN to huts near MAROEOIL STN. CAPT BENNETT, Staff Captain, remains at HOUVIN with Rear Hdqrs and 1st CDTM Bde. 1st CDA Hdqrs begins to function under 2nd Div Arty Hdqrs at 5pm: and controls 1st and 2nd Brigades CFA in the line.

Expected enemy bombardment failed to commence at 10.30pm.

According to reliable statements made by prisoners taken recently, enemy would launch an offensive with a 3-hour bombardment commencing at 10.30pm on the night of 9/10th May.

The ominous quiet which has prevailed recently and the fine weather leads to the belief that very shortly the enemy will "show his hand".

MAROEOIL May/10. Dull and very cool.

Night and early morning passed quietly. Light bombardment took place to the north but at a considerable distance from here.

CRA visits during the morning 1st and 2nd Brigade HQs and the batteries of the 2nd Bde.

Guns of the 5th and 7th Batteries are being moved to new locations during the night. 48th Howitzer Bty. is moving two howitzers back to its alternative position. The general idea in moving guns & howitzers is to prevent the enemy (in the event of his launching an attack) from smothering battery positions known to him with high explosive and gas.

The policy of moving guns forward for Tank defence after a hostile bombardment commenced was carefully looked into. It was thought that in the event of a hostile attack the chances of a gun "living" whilst being moved about by either man or animal were very few. Flank guns should be run out of their pits and used against Tanks from platforms prepared in the immediate battery locality.

MAROEOIL May/11. Dull and cool in morning, clearing to fine weather in afternoon.

CRA visits 1st Brigade main battery positions just east of ROCLINCOURT.

Rear Defensive lines, differing from those set forth by Canadian Corps, are ordered thru 15th Division. All lines of Defence are organized in Three Systems. 1st System includes TILLOY line and switches & lines EAST: 2nd System includes BLANGY line immediately East of ARRAS: 3rd System includes DAINVILLE lines about 2500 yds West of ARRAS. Switches at various points between these systems, recently dug by Canadian Corps, are stated to be in a derelict condition and if fought at all will probably be as an intermediate step between two of the different systems.

MAROEOIL May/12. Dull and cool.

CRA visits forward sections of 1st Bde and Tank Gun. Front remains rather ominously quiet.

Everyone is expecting an enemy blow on some portion of the front. Opinion seems to favor the "Drive" coming below ARRAS although a demonstration of sorts will be made probably north of BETHUNE.

Visibility very good from 5 – 8pm. Much aerial activity in this period. 1st CDAC move from CHAUSSÉE BRUNEHAUT to HABARCQ.

MAROEOIL May/13. Rain and wind.

CAPT BENNETT (Staff Captain) and remainder of 1st CDA Hdqrs move from HOUVIN and rejoin Headquarters at MAROEOIL.

Front was abnormally quiet during the entire day.

MAROEOIL May/14. Fine weather.

Few HV shells were fired into AGNEZ-LE-DUISANS during the early morning.

Much aerial activity thru out the day.

CRA visits Trench Mortar Brigade practicing at GIVENCY-LE-NOBLE. Morning series was finished and CRA did not wait for the afternoon practice. 6" Mortars were fired with no sub-bed on ordinary ground which was fairly soft. Apparently Mortars jumped considerably and would require heavy bed to prevent the jump.

MAROEOIL May/15. Fine weather.

CRA visits Field manoeuvres of 2nd Inf Bde in area near AVESNES-LES-COMPTE. For these operations artillery support was given by brigade of 4th CDA. Front remains very quiet.

Arrangements are completed for raid on enemy trenches near the "SNOUT" between GAVRELLE and FAMPOUX.

MAROEOIL May/16. Fine weather and extremely hot.

Raid made on enemy trenches at 3.45am by 13th Battn Royal Scots resulted in capture of 3 prisoners (normal). This raid was covered by 1st and 2nd Bdes CFA and 36th Bde RFA.

52nd Div Arty passed east thru AUBIGNY today. This may result in our relief in the very near future. Front remains exceptionally quiet in spite of the summer weather.

MAROEOIL May/17. Very fine weather.

Front remains very quiet. Slight increase in back area harassing fire. Considerable aerial activity during day and night. Bombs on AVESNES-LES-COMPTES and villages to south during the night.

MAROEOIL May/18. Fine weather continues. Extremely hot during the day.

Reconnaissance made of all defensive areas within Divisional boundaries. Front remains quiet with practically no hostile gas shelling.

There is further work to be done on the improvement of the effectiveness of heavy mortars, with particular emphasis on the possibility of making them more mobile. This is proving rather difficult.

MAROEOIL May/19. Fine and slightly cool.

Front quiet although enemy is increasing harassing fire against back areas.

CRA visits Trench Mortar demonstration at range near GIVENCHY LE NOBLE. Portable beds were tried out of various designs made by personnel of 1st CDTM Bde at SAVY workshops. All the beds, except the small one, shot the first few rounds rather well but in every case after four or five rounds shooting became so erratic that practice was stopped. General impression gained during the course of the afternoon was that for accurate shooting the sub-bed of 6" Newton would have to be of such a weight that it would be more or less immobile in any kind of offensive operations. All tests were carried out using 5th Charge which would probably be the only one of general use in supporting an advance in the later stages of the operation.

MAROEOIL May/20. Fine weather continues. Very hot.

This date was spoken of as the probable one for renewal of an offensive on a large scale. Nothing has developed and it is now said that offensive will probably commence within the next four days.

Prospective relief of 1st CDA will probably not take place in view of the fact that enemy action is expected. Front quiet.

MAROEOIL May/21. Fine weather. Heat is exceptional for this time of year.

Location of Hdqrs 1st CDA is rather ill-suited for comfort during hot period. It is in the first place alongside a railway line and railway yard and in the second the cantonment is of iron-roofed huts.

Reported that 5th CDA will relieve on 23rd, 24th and 25th. Orders are expected in the course of this day. Brigades on relief will proceed to BERLES and AUBIGNY. The latter area is considerable distance from Training area.

Efforts are being made to have this area exchanged for HERMAVILLE or TINCQUES.

Front quiet. Enemy harassing on rear areas slight.

MAROEOIL May/22. Fine weather.

Details of relief arrive from XVII Corps in which it is stated that guns will not be exchanged.

Battery Commanders of 5th CDA make a reconnaissance of the positions they will take over.

Considerable aerial activity during the day and night. Front remains quiet.

MAROEOIL May/23. Fine weather in early morning, later turning very cool and windy.

Very slight activity during the day on the front. 1st portion of relief – Forward sections – was carried out successfully before 11.30pm.

MAROEOIL 24/May. Rain and wind thru out the day.

5th CDA batteries arrive at wagon lines in preparation for taking over to-night. Suggested at one time that the march be made at an early hour during daylight to-morrow.

Weather is clearing towards evening and march will be carried out as previously arranged.

6-inch Howitzers mounted on rail carriages alongside a road. (*Courtesy of the RCA Museum*)

1st CDAC moves to ACQ. Good condition of horses and mules was remarked.

The move to Berles indicates that most of the Canadian Corps is to be concentrated in training areas well to the rear.

MAROEOIL May/25. Fair and cool.

1st & 2nd Brigades march – one at midnight and the other at 1am. Night march was carried out very satisfactorily, both brigades arriving at their billets in BERLES and HERMAVILLE before 5am.

Watering facilities at HERMAVILLE are very poor. The one pump in the town broke down early in the day after which watering was carried out 3 or 4 kilometres away. Endeavors are being made to get water in the town but the outlook is not good.

Billets in this town are much above the ordinary.

HQs 1st CDA move to BERLES Chateau from MAROEOIL station. This latter spot will probably have to be vacated by the 5th CDA HQs shortly as a 14" gun, the first of its kind it is said in France, is taking up a position on a spur close by.

Much "gunning" is heard during the early night.

From now on, the primary task of the Canadian Corps was to prepare to open the counter offensive when the German advance stalled through the overextension of its supply lines and attrition suffered by its forces over the last two months.

CHAPTER THREE

Preparation For Mobile Warfare

26 May – 31 July 1918

The Canadian Corps had already shown their capabilities in the first three years of the war. However, a new phase was about to open where much greater mobility would be the keynote for the success of its future operations; the guns of the Field Artillery in particular had to be repaired and maintained so that their accuracy could be relied on to direct fire just ahead of advancing infantry.

In July, the Corps was to be brought into action on the Lens/Arras Front. It appeared at first that this was in anticipation of a further thrust by the enemy. However, it turned out to be a subtle deception to encourage the enemy to believe that the Allied counter attack would be in the northern part of the sector. This deception was elaborated by sending contingents of signallers and medical staff northwards towards Flanders where their presence and signals traffic would falsely indicate the intentions of the Allied High Command.

Secrecy was all-important for the Allies because the Germans could concentrate their superior numbers in anticipation of any attack, should they be given notice of it. So the plan to mount the initial counter attack on the Amiens front had to be hidden until the last possible moment. The Canadian Corps' reputation for spearheading successful operations meant that it was vital that no reports of its movement to the Amiens Front reached the Germans.

------oOo------

Diaries for 26 May 1918 Onwards

BERLES May/26. Fine weather although dull at odd periods thru the day.

CRA visits 1st Brigade batteries and 2nd Bde HQs during the morning.

"Trench Mortars" give new sub-bed a trial at GIVENCHY. With a few slight alterations this bed ought to be satisfactory. Over 20 rnds were fired at 5th Charge with very few bad shots, these being due most probably to faulty ammunition rather than defects in the bed. An "all iron" bed was tried but was not a success.

The trials intending to find a solution to the difficulty of moving heavy mortars in support of mobile infantry are less successful than had been hoped.

Trials of different kinds of ammunition used by field artillery were essential in order to find out whether or not shrapnel was more useful in mobile warfare. High explosive shells made craters in the field of battle that would hinder the advance of tanks and impede the rapid movement of infantry.

BERLES May/27. Fine weather.

1st Brigade guns are calibrated at PETAWAWA Range east of GOUY SERVINS.

Ten officers from brigades proceed by bus to demonstration near WESTREHEM of the killing power of the H.E. and Shrapnel (18pdr). CRA and Lt Col PIERCEY attend this demonstration by car. Demonstration was carried out at 3000 and 5000 yards range. 18pdr shrapnel was shown to be much superior to H.E. (106 fuze) against targets in the open.

Rumors are afloat re enemy "Drive" between SOISSONS & RHEIMS.

The long-awaited German offensive materialises away from the Lens/Arras area between Soissons and Rheims. It has some success in advancing on a wide front. Meanwhile, the 1st, 3rd and 4th Divisions are being prepared for the anticipated Allied counter offensive.

BERLES May/28. Fair and Cool.

CRA visits XVIII Corps R.A. regarding what artillery could be given from XVIII Corps to help in counter attack by 1st Can Division on ST CATHERINE Switch or ECURIE Switch. As both of these switches lie more or less between the XVII and XVIII Corps it is rather difficult to arrange any definite artillery support beyond that which would be given by our own brigades.

Enemy have penetrated about ten miles on an 18 mile front between SOISSONS and RHEIMS. This explains the unusual amount of harassing fire by HV guns on towns well behind our lines.

Front in ARRAS area remains fairly quiet.

An important part of the preparation of the artillery is the recalibration of their field guns. This is done at the Petawawa calibration range. Each gun fires standard rounds of ammunition through two screens placed well apart so that the speed of the shells can be accurately measured using an electric timer. This enables the gun to have its own ranging figures that should be used when it is being fired. Firing many rounds wears the barrel making this recalibration essential in order to maintain the greatest possible accuracy. This is doubly important when the infantry is called on to advance close to the falling shells.

BERLES May/29. Fine weather.

Visit paid to PETAWAWA Calibration Range near GOUY SERVINS while 2nd Bde guns are being calibrated. This appears quite a "well run" organization.

Preparations are being made for inspection by Corps Commander & G.O.C. on Friday. Difficulty is being experienced in locating fields large enough to hold a brigade in line at half interval.

Training and experimentation with new, more portable beds for mortars is not very successful and further work is needed. However, the use of trench mortars is clearly likely to be very successful if they can be more flexibly deployed in battle conditions. Furthermore, the maintenance and recalibration of field guns, after their recent intensive use, is being carried out.

Further problems are being encountered in the development of improved 'beds' for heavy mortars.

BERLES May/30. Fair and cool.

1st Cdn Div T.M. Bde gave another demonstration in firing with a portable bed at ranges at GIVENCHY LE NOBLE. One bed stood firing of 25 bombs but after that began to shoot erratic. It seems to be rather well demonstrated from experience within the last three weeks that it is possible to make a bed which will "stand up" for the first twenty or twenty five rds at fourth or fifth charges but beyond that number it is almost impossible. In an offensive operation it could be stated that the majority of tasks (destroyed strong point in Farm House etc) could be accomplished with forty or fifty rounds from a pair of 6" Newtons.

General Currie has been successful in retrieving command of three of his four divisions now that they are mainly being held in reserve. He has been

Lieutenant General Sir Arthur Currie, GOC Canadian Corps, salutes as he reviews a Canadian Siege Battery equipped with 6-inch Howitzers. Second from the left, also wearing a red and white brassard on his arm, is Brigadier General E. W. B. 'Dinky' Morrison, GOC RA Canadian Corps. Eight Canadian Siege Batteries in the Canadian Corps Heavy Artillery were equipped with 6-inch Howitzers. (*Courtesy of the RCA Museum*)

able to convince GHQ that the Canadian divisions have demonstrated their success in overcoming the enemy at Vimy, Hill 70 and Passchendaele when acting in concert. Being able to train together under Currie's command for future battles is a great boost for the Canadian troops' morale.

BERLES May/31. Very fine weather.

Inspection of 1st CDA (less DAC) by Lieut Gen Sir A W Currie Cdg Cdn Corps & Major Gen. A C Macdonell Cdg 1st Cdn Div, GOC RA Can Corps was present.

Inspecting officers were very pleased with the entire showing and particularly with Trench Mortars and 5th Battery CFA. 2nd Bde HQs entertained at tea following completion of Inspection.

Diaries for June 1918

After a somewhat acrimonious series of exchanges with Allied High command and Canadian Government representatives in London, General Currie GOC Canadian Corps had the 1st, 3rd and 4th Canadian Divisions once more under his command. The fact that they were in reserve and under a training regime in preparation for open warfare was significant. However, the 2nd Canadian Division remained in the line to the south as part of the VI Corps under command of the 3rd (British) Army.

For the parts of the Canadian Corps under General Currie's command, the month of June opens with a well-organised series of inter-divisional sporting events. The 1st Battery CFA also held a dinner for its officers, including the following individuals: Col. C. H. L. Sharman; Major L. C. Goodeve, Brigade Major 4th Divisional Artillery; Major R. G. Thackray, DAQMG, Canadian Corps; Major A. H. Bick, Brigade Major 1st Canadian Divisional Artillery, who came over as a junior officer with the first contingent in 1914; and Major H. T. C. Whitley, currently commander of the 1st Battery.

Throughout the month, the emphasis was to be on training, but clearly there was also the need to maintain physical fitness. Sports were encouraged as much as possible and were organised not only as a diversion and recreation, but also to improve physical fitness of all ranks.

BERLES June/1. Fine Weather.

Slight increase in activity during morning in the direction of ARRAS – LENS – probably in accordance with enemy orders captured recently stating that every endeavor should be made to force the British to hold reserves behind the whole line.

Units carry out elimination contests for mounted sports to be held tomorrow.

BERLES June/2. Fine weather.

Heavy firing heard at odd intervals from ARRAS – LENS direction.

Sports [events] were carried out very successfully. The Divisional Commander and several CRAs were present & many officers from the 1st Division infantry & Artillery officers from all divisions of Canadian Corps & adjoining Corps.

The Brigade Major [A.H.B.] went on leave & Major C V Stockwell took over his duties during his absence.

BERLES June/3. Fine weather.

Artillery activity around ARRAS much decreased. Very quiet day.

2nd Bde marched to CHELERS training area for manoeuvres.

BERLES June/4. Fine weather.

CRA watched manoeuvres of 2nd Bde during afternoon.

German bombing planes dropped bombs close to SAVY shaking houses in BERLES about 12.30 am.

BERLES June/5. Very fine weather.

No sound of bombardment from direction of ARRAS. 1st Bde CFA went to manoeuvre area to stay for 48 hours.

BERLES June/6. Very fine weather.

1st Bde carried out Brigade training in MAGNICOURT area. CRA watched the afternoon exercise. News of fighting in SOUTH very meagre, but Germans seem to be held.

BERLES June/7. Weather Fine.

Very Quiet day. 2nd Bde carried out battery manoeuvres in MINGOVAL and MAGNICOURT areas.

BERLES June/8. Fine weather.

2nd Bde carried out battery manoeuvres in MAGNICOURT area. C.R.A. watched manoeuvres and presented ribbon of D.C.M. to QMS HYMAN 48th Howitzer Battery.

BERLES June/9. Fine weather. Very quiet.

BERLES June/10. Slight rain in early morning, cleared up & fine by noon.

Everything very quiet. 1st Bde carried out Brigade training in morning in MAGNICOURT area, owing to fact that 4th Canadian Div have use of training area on Tuesdays and Fridays. 1st Bde could not billet on area on night of 10/11 as intended.

BERLES June/11. Showery in morning, cleared up by noon.

1st Canadian Divisional Signals gave a demonstration with message carrying rockets; most of the 1st CDA officers attended; rockets seemed on the whole satisfactory.

BERLES June/12. Very fine weather.

AM: 2nd Bde carried out skeleton scheme in MONCHY BRETON area. It was rather interfered with by a scheme of 3rd C.I.B. employing tanks.

PM: D.A.C. had sports; very successful meeting; GOC was present for the latter portion.

BERLES Jun/13. Weather fair, rather cloudy.

PM: Divisional Artillery Elimination Sports were carried out. Everything very successful. Large number of events were won by officers. The TMs were also to the fore.

The Canadian Corps had no tanks of their own, although they were proving increasingly effective in giving mobile support for the infantry by carrying heavy armaments. They were also useful in breaching many existing defensive measures such as barbed wire and trenches. It was essential for artillery officers to gain experience of their uses in battle conditions. Some brigades of tanks were to be placed under Canadian command and prove useful during many of the battles later in 1918.

BERLES June/14.

AM: Arrangements for tactical scheme with 1st C.I.B.[Canadian Infantry Brigade] and tanks were gone into; there was a conference of umpires on the ground.

PM: C.R.A. & officers 1st Bde CFA attended a demonstration by tanks [finding them] very interesting; it was noticed what an improvement had been made in them; they turned so much quicker & were handier in every way than the old ones. A most effective smoke screen was put up by one tank; another special tank went over a trench 13 feet wide. MKV, whippet and supply tanks all took part in demonstration; a very large number of officers were present.

BERLES June/15. Very fine but colder.

2nd Bde took part in tactical exercise with 1st C.I.B.; many lessons were learnt & the difficulties of cooperation of infantry with artillery & the necessity of much practice in it was clearly shown.

Trial was made of bringing up forward guns with tanks. The experiment was not altogether a success.

Elimination for Divisional sports, D.A.C. got into the final of Baseball.

Competitive sports events are organised to improve fitness and morale. German bombing from the air can only be carried out at night because Allied aerial strength makes their bomber aircraft too vulnerable in daylight hours.

BERLES June/16. Showery.

Elimination in boxing of Divisional Sports. Bombs dropped around BERLES about midnight; no damage.

BERLES June/17. Fine till about 4.30pm.

Divisional Sports; Very successful meet; CDA were second in Divisional Group winners; D.A.C. won divisional baseball championship.

CRA leaves for England on 14 days leave. Brigade Major [A.H.B.] returns from leave.

BERLES June/18. Showery. Weather appears to have broken.

Lieut Col S B ANDERSON DSO arrives and will be CRA 1st CDA during Brig Gen Thacker's absence.

All units carried out training in vicinity of wagon lines.

Orders are received for tactical exercise between 2nd Can Inf Bde and 1st C.E. Bde [Canadian Engineers]. Artillery support will be given by elements of 1st Bde CFA. This exercise will take place on Friday June 21st.

BERLES June/19. Rain during most of day.

Finals in Divisional Tennis Tournament are being held at VILLERS CHATEL. Div Arty has one in Singles and several teams in doubles for semi finals.

Final arrangements are being made for scheme on 21st.

BERLES June/20. Fair and cool. Showery towards evening.

Artillery supporting RED Force moved out during morning to area north of MAGNICOURT to be in position for Exercise tomorrow. The artillery consists of 1st and 4th Batteries and ½ 2nd How Bty under command of Lieut Col Piercy DSO.

Rain began about six pm which necessitated postponement of Tactical Exercise to Monday. This is partly due to appraisement of damage done to crops in training area being carried on at present by French Government and military agents.

BERLES June/21. Fair and showery at times.

RED Force artillery return to billets at BERLES area.

General news regarding Italian front seems to be quite satisfactory – the Italians are looking good in their offensive along the PIAVE sector.

BERLES June/22. Cool and showery.

Three officers from each artillery brigade are taken up in observation balloon for instruction at BRETENCOURT.

CAPT H W TAYLOR supernumery captain in 1st Brigade is posted to 5th Bde CFA 2nd CDA. CAPT R S HAYES goes to 2nd Bde CFA.

Conference held at HQs of all unit Commanders to enquire into the efficiency of our present anti-gas measures. It was found from the opinions expressed that improvements could be made viz.

1. All ranks will go thru gas chamber under direct supervision of a qualified gas officer at least once every 3 weeks.

2. All Gas Officers thru out the formations will meet Div Arty Gas Officer periodically to discuss bettering the existing system.

3. Lectures will be [given] from time to time by Gas Officers from HQs Div. Corps and Army.

BERLES June/23. Fair with slight showers at intervals.

Notice received that no large schemes will be undertaken. This cancels the scheme arranged for tomorrow.

Training being carried on in wagon line area by all units.

Reunion dinner held at 2nd Bde HQs HERMAVILLE of all old 2nd Bde officers.

BERLES June/24. Rain clearing toward evening. Very windy.

Much difficulty is being experienced in getting practice flights in balloon by officers of units. Two days now allotted by Division have been so windy with rain squalls that no balloon ascension could be made.

All signallers in CCRC will from now be kept at Reinforcement Depot AUBIN ST VAAST. This arrangement was due to Col SHARMAN's visit to France. He found that even when signallers were being sent over regularly enough when they arrived at the units they had lost most of their knowledge of signalling. At this depot they will be kept fresh with continuous signalling exercises.

BERLES June/25. Fine with light clouds.

Lt Col ANDERSON acting CRA pays visit to 1st Army School Tactical exercise. A few points of special interest were observed. The scheme was one of ADVANCE and was carried out in skeleton. Great attention was given to the Officers Patrol. Artillery Officers in addition to FOOs were sent forward for the sole purpose of collecting and sending back all information regarding the situation from the infantry in the line. This will be given a trial in the very near future by the brigades on our training area.

2nd Can Div in the line between ARRAS and ALBERT is being relieved by 3rd Can Div tonight. Area occupied by 3rd CDiv is being handed over to 74th Division and 2nd Can Div occupy area south east of ST POL while in rest.

BERLES June/26. Cloudy but clearing to fine weather later in day.

2nd How Battery & 4th Battery carry out successful morning's work with aeroplane on training area at MONCHY BRETON. Reading of ground strips sending LL, GF & NF calls, Spotting Batteries etc were carried out.

Ammunition expert is delivering lectures to brigades and DAC in turn.

BERLES June/27. Fine weather.

7th Battery & 48th How Battery conduct morning's exercise with aeroplane.

GOC 1st Can Div delivers very instructive talk to all officers of 1st Can Div Arty at HQs BERLES in afternoon. Discipline and art of command were topics emphasized and done in such a way that only he can do.

One section 18pdrs cooperate in scheme of 7th Can Inf Battn during the day. (2nd Bde – 6th Battery)

BERLES June/28. Fine weather.

Arrangements made for one company 8th Battn to represent infantry outpost line in tactical exercise scheduled for tomorrow.

1st CDAC made a further step to Can Corps Baseball championship. DAC team won from 26th Battn (2nd Can Div) by score of 5 – 0 at CHATEAU DE LA HAIE grounds.

The use of telephone (wired) communication was clearly not a practical option in open warfare conditions when relocation of batteries was too frequent to allow installation of fixed wiring. However, training was needed to ensure that new methods could be used effectively under battle conditions.

BERLES June/29. Fine weather, threatening rain at intervals in afternoon.

Tactical exercise is carried out on MONCHY BRETON Training area by 1st Bde CFA. Officers of 2nd Bde acted as umpires. Scheme went rather slow in the Initial stages due to 4th Can Div Scheme which was on the ground of jumping off line. Communication thru out was very poor partly due to the fact that only visible and wireless were allowed for the first time. The main idea in the scheme was practice in the use of Artillery Officers Patrols collecting all information from Infantry in the line and sending messages back at odd intervals to the Forward Signal Centre of the Battery. This novel feature together with the fact that no telephones were allowed was the cause of the exercise not being a success.

Lecture on Tank Cooperation in future offensives was given at HOUDAIN. Experiments carried out quite recently in Wireless Telephones have shown that the scope for action of tanks will be almost unlimited. More work with tanks in our exercises will now probably be advocated.

BERLES June/30. Fine weather.

Final preparations being made for Corps Sports to be held at TINCQUES tomorrow July 1st. It promises to be one of the greatest events of its kind ever held.

Rehearsal for Tactical Exercise is carried out at MONCHY BRETON Training Area. One section 18pdrs is taking part. It will be carried out probably during the next week with the Corps Commander in attendance.

Diaries for July 1918

The month opened with a celebration parade marking Dominion Day. Nearly 50,000 Canadian soldiers of all ranks were assembled at Tincques, a village 14 miles west of Arras, in perfect weather. The Canadian Corps had continued their sporting activities, with the finals of many events taking place. The Duke of Connaught, the Governor General of Canada, took the salute of the assembled ranks of all available members of the Corps. Sir Robert Borden, the Prime Minister, and his Cabinet Ministers were also present. It is hard to imagine how this event, involving large numbers of troops on parade not very far from the battle front, could have been carried out without local air superiority during daylight hours.

General Currie had now taken charge of the 2nd Canadian Division, which until recently had been in the line under the command of the (British) VI Corps. This move brought all four Canadian Divisions under Currie's direct command for the first time since the enemy offensive opened on 21 March.

Later in the month, all four divisions of the Corps would engage in the fighting once again with their relief of the British XVII Corps in the line.

The important longer-term role of the Canadian Corps would become clearer as the month drew to a close.

BERLES July/1. Fine weather and rather hot.

In accordance with Corps Commander's Special Order, all ranks of 1st CDA took a holiday to-day as the tactical situation permitted. Corps Sports were held at TINCQUES beginning quite early (10am). Practically every Division in 1st Army and many of 3rd Army were represented in attendance. Organization was good, as delays seen frequently in Field Days of this description were nil. 1st Can Div very nearly doubled the total number of points gained by any other Division of the Corps; thereby showing the superiority of the "Little Old Red Patch" in Sport as well as in the harder work of war.

BERLES July/2. Fine weather continues. Roads very dusty. Need of rain being felt thru out country.

Another rehearsal (2nd) is held on MONCHY BRETON Area in demonstration of infiltration methods used to such good effect by the enemy. Smoke bombs were used to indicate firing of 18pdrs. This smoke demonstration suggested the possibility of screening 18pdr sniping guns with smoke. This matter will be given a trial in the near future.

CRA returns from English leave.

BERLES July/3. Fine weather. Light clouds and threatening rain at odd intervals towards evening.

Two batteries 1st Bde CFA worked with contact plane on BERTHONSART area during morning.

Brig Gen THACKER is acting GOC Division during to-day and to-morrow while GOC is inspecting Cavalry Corps School and making arrangements for the opening of School of Equitation at Can Corps

Training continues with emphasis on gas warfare. The first signs of an influenza epidemic, mild at this stage, begin to take effect.

BERLES July/4. Fine weather but rather windy.

CRA attends School gas lecture at 1st Bde – Attendance not quite up to the mark owing to sickness. Epidemic of what is called Influenza, Spanish Fever or Bolshevism seems to be dying out very slowly. As yet none have taken this twice and as it is only 4 or 5 days duration it will not take long to "go thru" the whole Div Arty.

BERLES July/5. Dull with no rain.

Tactical exercise is carried out before Corps Commander [General A. W. Currie] and representatives from the four Canadian Divisions. It was to demonstrate the '"Infiltration" method of advance, supported by tanks L. & Medium Trench mortars and forward 18pdrs.

General discussion took place at conference following the exercise – main topic being the use of smoke which was thought to have been overdone in this instance. This was probably traceable to the 18pdrs which used smoke bombs to represent the gun firing. One use of smoke bomb which suggested itself from an artillery point of view was that of screening the teams limbering up in an advance or retirement. This could be easily done as was shown this morning.

BERLES July/6. Fine weather.

Conference regarding 1st Inf Bde Tactical Exercise is held at 2nd Bttn HQs ANZIN near ARRAS. This will be carried out on Tuesday afternoon in area between BRUNEHAUT Corner and ECURIE. Two 18pdrs and two 6" Newtons are required.

1st CDA Gymkana is held during afternoon in Chateau grounds BERLES. 3rd Battery CFA win unit championship by combined individual effort of all 3rd Bty Officers. Several outside umpires officiated including Major A PATTINSON DSO from 2nd Cdn Div.

BERLES July/7. Fine weather and very warm.

Conference regarding exercise of 3rd Can Inf Bde held at 13th Battn HQs CAUCOURT where all arrangements are made. Rather new role for Forward Guns and Trench Mortars will be tried out.

Ramming home a shell in a 6-inch howitzer. (*Courtesy of the RCA Museum*)

Warning Order received with details of relief of XVIII Corps by Can Corps during next week. 1st Can Division will hold sector astride RIVER SCARPE.

This will be the first occasion when all four divisions of the Canadian Corps can be deployed as a joint force since the enemy offensive began on 21 March.

BERLES July/8. Dull and very sultry.

Tactical Exercise on Monchy Breton Area was more or less a failure. Inf. flanks kept on advancing in spite of the fact that m.g. nest in centre was firing enfilade on all attacking line. Artillery were not called into action at all. Corps Commander explains mistakes pointing out lessons which should be learned and impresses on all ranks that this is probably only due to "staleness" which ought to be rectified within the next week as the Can Corps is going in to fight the enemy with new vigor and determination and with the latest atrocities (bombing hospitals and sinking hospital ships) ever in their minds.

Trench Mortar demonstration will be carried out to-morrow at LA COMTE – about ten teams are taking part.

BERLES July/9. Fine weather during morning but turning to rain in afternoon.

Trench Mortar demonstration held by First Army at LA COMTE. Entries from majority of Divisions in First Army. 1st CDA entry was unfortunate in time – ground very hard which delayed the putting down of bed and several unlucky delays caused a very bad showing as compared with several other DAs which had no sub bed at all. Beds will be given an exhaustive test at T.M. School. From these tests a standard bed will be chosen.

BERLES July/10. Showery.

CRA visits 15th DA & 56th DA reference relief. 1st Cdn Division will hold practically all present 15th Division Sector together with about one half 56th Division. Field Artillery covering Division will be 1st Cdn Div Arty and two Army Brigades now in position south of the River SCARPE.

Divisional Hdqrs will be at ETRUN for the present and will probably move to DUISANS when Can Corps Hdqrs moves to GIVENCHY LE NOBLE.

BERLES July/11. Showery.

Capt KITTSON 3rd Battery goes to hospital. 1st Bde CFA is running low in number of officers. Within the past week Lieut DA ANDERSON and Lieut MILLIDGE both of 1st Battery gone to hospital.

Divisional boundaries in new area are constantly changing – two changes being received within the last 24 hours.

BERLES July/12. Rain clearing towards evening.

Brigade Commanders and DTMO go forward to make a reconnaissance of new area.

Field artillery available for covering the 1st Can Div will be 4 brigades – for SOS purposes, frontage per 18pdr will be 67 yards. SOS line will probably be in bits with concentrations covering important tactical points.

BERLES July/13. Showery weather.

Inspection of Signal Sections of 1st CDA is made by CRA with satisfactory results.

Advance parties of 15th Scottish Division arrive in this area. Rumors are afloat that 1st CDA will have to evacuate present billets by noon to-morrow.

The situation during the relief period remains uncertain with the intentions of the enemy far from clear. The disposition of artillery units particularly seems to be changing constantly. The general situation on the Western Front is shown in Map 3. The enemy penetration is far greater to the south where a breakthrough could threaten to reach the channel coast.

BERLES/AUBIGNY July/14. Showery.

1st & 2nd Brigades ordered out of billets in rear areas, and march to vicinity of wagon lines which they will take over to-morrow. Majority of batteries bivouac in open fields. Bde Headquarters are accommodated in ETRUN. Hdqrs of 1st CDA move to chateau at AUBIGNY.

AUBIGNY July/15. Dull weather and very hot & sultry.

Relief of batteries of 15 Div Arty is complete by 11pm. 1st CDAC move from ACQ to GOUVES. 1st CDTM Bde from AGNIERES to ANZIN. 15th Div Artillery receive orders to entrain on 16th (to-morrow). Their destination will probably be near PARIS to assist in repelling the latest drive of the enemy between CHATEAU THIEARREY and the ARGONNE.

Warning order issued that 16th Div Arty will relieve 277th & 311th Bde which are now supporting half the 1st Can Div in the line.

AUBIGNY/ETRUN July/16. Fair weather thru out the day, but violent electrical storms between 1 and 7am.

HQs 1st CDA relieve 15th DA at 10am.

Everything smoothes out very quickly in the new headquarters.

Warning order received yesterday is confirmed today. The CRA 16th Division arrives to look things over. They intend to stage at FREVIN CAPELLE on the way down to this area from their present area near PERNES.

ETRUN July/17. Dull and Sultry.

First Sections 16th Divn Arty relieve sections of 311 and 277 AFA Brigades RFA holding the line immediately south of the SCARPE. No headquarters is available at present for 16th DA hdqrs.

The arrangement which was in effect when the two army brigades were in the line will hold good viz. the senior brigade commander taking command of the two brigades which form one group covering one infantry brigade.

Deception is a key element in the first stages of the counter offensive, in which the Canadian Corps is to form the spearhead. The Canadians are very active in their present position near the Arras Front to make the Germans believe that this is where the initial counter attacks will be launched.

ETRUN July/18. Fair weather.

Relief of 311 and 277 AFA Brigades is completed by 177 and 180 Brigades RFA belonging to 16th Div Arty.

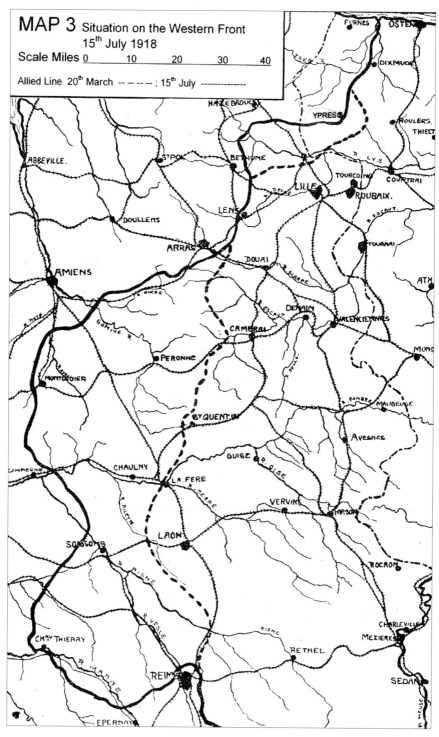

Situation on the Western Front, 15 July 1918.

New changes in disposition are received. 2nd Canadian Div on our right is ordered out of the line; 3rd Can inf Bde is carrying out relief of 2nd Can Div infantry to-night. On completion of relief 56th Div Arty together with 8th AFA Bde CFA (which is not yet in action) come under control of CRA 1st Cdn Div. This disposition gives 1st Cdn Div all three Infantry Bdes in the line supported by 7 brigades of Field Artillery.

Warning is now received that to-morrow night 4th Can Division on our left is extending down to River SCARPE taking control of our two artillery brigades. Changes in disposition appear to be uppermost for the past two days – no time being allowed to get settled in one place before moving on to the next.

ETRUN July/19. Fair weather.

At 6am the 56th DA and 8th AFA Bde passed to control of 1st Can Div. 8th AFA Bde is making a reconnaissance of areas immediately south east of ARRAS during the day and will take up position to-night. They will be in silent positions and covering the TELEGRAPH HILL – NEUVILLE VITASSE Section.

Warning received that 311 and 277 AFA Bdes RFA will relieve 56th DA commencing night 20/21st.

ETRUN July/20. Showery weather.

First Sections of 277 and 311 AFA Bdes RFA relieve Forward Sections of 56th Div Arty in Right Section (TELEGRAPH HILL) 1st Can Division.

Front remains extremely quiet during all these changes. At 6am 1st and 2nd Bdes CFA covering FAMPOUX Section passed to command of CRA 4th Cdn Div. 1st Cdn Division had three Infantry brigades in the line covered by 7 brigades of Field Artillery. Northern Boundary of 1st Cdn Division is now River SCARPE.

It is thought that the latest redistribution will be only temporary as 3rd Division will probably sideslip to the north taking over our Right Brigade (Infantry) frontage and that 1st Cdn Division will in a few days be astride River SCARPE again.

Several Gas projections are contemplated and will be carried out as soon as favorable wind presents itself.

ETRUN July/21. Rain thru out morning, clearing toward evening.

The Two Army Brigades complete the relief of 56th Div Arty and form Right Group 1st CDA under command of Col COCHRANE OC 277th AFA Bde RFA. 56th DA Batteries are bivouacking alongside their wagon lines for the night and will march to-morrow morning to FREVIN CAPELLE Area with DA Hdqrs at CHATEAU AUBIGNY.

As moves have more or less ceased, Divisional Defence Schemes are being worked on with great energy.

The Canadian Corps is at last in the line again as a fighting entity. However, there is much uncertainty about the intentions of the enemy. It still seems to be highly likely that they will renew their offensive operations. The result is that the Allied forces are being moved about as threats are perceived in different parts of the front.

ETRUN July/22. Fair but windy and turning cooler.

Warning Order received that on 23rd/24th 1st Can Div takes over north brigade (Infantry) of 3rd Can Division to our right. This means the upsetting once again of arrangements for Defence. Artillery covering this Section will probably be two Army Brigades.

ETRUN July/23. Fair weather.

Heavy gunfire was heard to the south from early morning until daybreak when it died away – probably a raid on large scale by NEW ZEALANDERS who have been making progress near HEBUTERNE. Before the North Brigade 3rd Can Division passes to 1st Can Division there is a inter relief of 175th AFA Bde and 181st AFA Bde RFA. (175th coming over to the front taken over by the 1st Can Division). Inter relief beginning to-day of 1st & 2nd Bdes CFA now covering Brigade in TELEGRAPH HILL Section. This inter relief will be completed by 24th.

ETRUN July/24. Showery.

At 6am Divisional Sector extends as far south as MERCATEL. 1st Can Inf Bde relieved 9th Can Inf Bde (3rd Cdn Division). This new section will be covered by two artillery brigades, at present 10th Bde CFA and 175th AFA Bde RFA. 10th Bde CFA is however being relieved; relief to be completed 25/26th, by 282nd AFA Bde RFA – a brigade which has only last night arrived in this area from HOUDAIN where it was resting after being engaged in the FORÊT NIEPPE operation of several weeks ago. Inter relief between 1st & 2nd Bdes CFA and 311 and 277 AFA Bdes is completed at 4pm.

Our brigades go into practically the same positions which they handed over to 56th Div Arty on the 9th April.

ETRUN July/25. Very windy with rain at intervals.

Tank demonstration given by Australians near AMIENS was attended by many Canadian officers. Demonstration was considered quite a success and more or less showed the great use of the Mark V Tank. Relief of 10th Bde CFA by 282nd AFA Bde RFA is completed by 11pm.

System of Defence on 3rd Can Division Front was entirely different to the one employed by Can Corps: -

1. SOS searched forward 200 yards instead of remaining stationary.

A 6-inch Howitzer under a cam net. (*Courtesy of the RCA Museum*)

2. Main line of Resistance is the 3rd line of Defence from the front line and not the 2nd as it is here.

3. Chief Defence will apparently be made on a line which joins the DAINVILLE line in Can Corps area about 5500 yds behind Outpost Line.

Along this latter line 6" Newtons were distributed in Defensive Positions. Only one 6" Newton and one 9.45 HTM were taken over by 1st Can Div. Newtons in Defensive positions were taken out by 3rd CDTM Bde.

All preparations for large scale raids are being made on the various Inf Bde Sections. 2nd Can Inf Bde will raid in vicinity of BROKEN MLL north east of TILLOY LEZ MAFFLAINES to-morrow with 5th & 10th Battns.

ETRUN July/26. Showery.

Several changes are being made in the arrangements for 2nd Bde (Infantry) Raid. Smoke Barrage is thought to be rather far East and one 4.5 Howitzer is placed on another point.

Raid is carried out at 9.00am. Weather is very bad. Smoke barrage is scarcely required as darkness almost hides the raiders. Artillery barrage is considered very effective. Seven prisoners result. Normal identification. Visit paid to 16th Battn Hdqrs TILLOY to arrange about raid which will be made to-morrow night.

Demonstration in conjunction with 2nd Bde Raid is made on part to be raided to-morrow. This may help to deceive the Boche as TMs have been cutting wire at this point during the day, but nothing will be done to-morrow.

ETRUN July/27. Rain and wind during the whole day at intervals; but clearer after 4pm.

Enemy retaliation during last night's raid was very weak – credit for which may be given to our "COUNTER" (Can Corps Heavy Arty Counter Battery STAFF). What shelling there was appeared to be done by Boche Flanking Artilleries as only targets were shelled which would normally be given supporting artillery.

Registration checking is carried out by batteries engaged in to-night's raid. In order to get satisfactory results OPs were established in PELVES ALLEY and trees in TILLOY WOOD.

Raid will take place at 12.50am to-morrow morning.

ETRUN July/28. Fair weather.

Identifications secured in raid early this morning were normal – one machine gun and one dead Boche were taken. Difficulty was experienced by infantry in Left raid on STONE DUMP due to causes as yet unknown. Investigation will be made to-morrow or day following both from artillery and infantry points of view.

Warning order received that Can Corps in the line will be relieved in the course of the next few days and held in GHQ Reserve in First Army ready to move to Second Army. This will complete a two-weeks tour in the line which has been filled with changes of one kind or another.

ETRUN July/29. Fine weather in the morning, showers in the afternoon. Misty.

CRA visits Tank demonstration given by Australians near AMIENS. It was practically the same experimenting as 1st Can Div engaged in while in Training during May and June and therefore did not present the novel characteristics which it was claimed it would.

8th AFA Bde RFA withdraw to wagon lines and are preparing to entrain to-morrow at AUBIGNY and SAVY BERLETTE for a destination which cannot be found on LENS II or AMIENS sheets ("BACQUEL").

ETRUN July/30. Misty weather but no rain.

Conference of CRAs at RA HQs DUISANS at 8.30am. CRA visits 2nd Bde CFA HQs to look into the misunderstanding between 3rd Can Inf Bde and artillery engaged in raid on STONE DUMP and enemy posts on early morning of 28th July. From an artillery standpoint everything appears satisfactory which is borne out later in the day by a repetition of all barrages as they were during actual raid with corrections made for differences in barometer, temperature and wind. The whole question is one more or less mathematical certainty against a human uncertainty – the proof of one however is not convincing to those supporting the other view.

175th Army Brigade RFA will be withdrawn to GHQ Reserve. This will necessitate a rearrangement for artillery supporting the Front about the night of 1st/2nd August. Another change will be necessary on the morning of 2nd August when 56th Division take over most of our present Divisional Sector with only four brigades of artillery in support.

Order is issued regarding relief of 1st CDA by 56th Div Arty on nights July 31st/1st August and August 1st/2nd. 1st CDA on relief will go to HOUVIN area with HQs at Chateau HOUVIN HOUVIGNEUL. March will be made on 2nd August by brigades and 1st CDTM Bde. (1st CDAC moving on 1st August)

Many rumors as to our destination are afloat. It is reported that 2 battalions of Canadians entrained for the north several days ago. However, 8th Arty Brigade CFA proceeded by train to a destination in vicinity of AMIENS. Can Corps HQs moved away to destination unknown to-day. XVII Corps are now functioning at DUISANS.

Preparations for a counter offensive by the Allies are being carried out in great secrecy. The Canadians particularly are being warned to 'Keep their mouths shut', with notices in their Pay Books to this effect. The intention of the High Command is to redeploy the Canadian Corps as the spearhead of the counter attack near Amiens. However, in order to ensure that the enemy does not realise that this is their intention, two battalions of Canadian signals and support troops are sent north towards the Ypres sector. Signals will be sent by these units while they are moving north to confuse the Germans.

ETRUN July/31. Fine weather. Misty.

When 56th Div Arty assumes command on morning 2nd August, there will be four brigades of Field Artillery covering their Front – Right Group less 175 Army Brigade RFA, Centre Group composed of 56th DA – and Left Group less 180th Bde RFA. 177th Bde RFA remaining brigade of present Left group is passing to command of CRA 57th Division (Centre Division XVII Corps).

Due to rumors of our entraining on night 2nd/3rd August it is decided to have our brigades move to HOUVIN area on 1st August – guns and remaining transport required to complete relief on night 1st/2nd August moving as soon as relief is complete.

Extensive hostile bombing over back areas during first portion of night.

The Canadian Corps will now move to undertake their role in the counter attack on the unsuspecting enemy on the front west of Amiens. This move will be carried out in great secrecy, under cover of darkness as far as possible. All possible means are employed to keep this information from the enemy, including flying noisy aircraft over the area to cover the noises of tank and truck movements on the ground. The areas in which the Canadian Corps concentrated in preparation for the counter attack on the Amiens Front are shown in Map 4.

CHAPTER FOUR

The Grand Offensive is Launched

The Battle of Amiens, 1 August – 20 August 1918

In great secrecy and under cover of darkness where possible, the Canadian Corps moved into offensive positions, ready to attack the unsuspecting enemy on the front west of Amiens. Because the Canadian Corps had already been employed to spearhead so many successful assaults, the enemy would immediately suspect that the counter offensive would begin at Amiens, and not the northern sector near Ypres as they had been led to believe, if the reports of the Canadian movements got out. On this occasion the Australian Corps would also be employed for the attack, with each corps reinforced by a British Division. Earlier in July, the French armies had achieved a notable victory further south, driving back the enemy from where they had been threatening Paris from positions on the River Marne.

The cross-country movement of men and equipment over a distance of approximately 40 miles from Arras to Amiens began in great secrecy on 31 July. To carry out such a large-scale movement in the hours of darkness, without attracting the unwelcome attention of the enemy, was itself a remarkable achievement; the artillery alone was taken in thirteen trains. Furthermore, the build-up of men and equipment in a concentrated area near Amiens for the opening of the assault also had to be controlled in a similarly concealed manner. Bad weather hindered enemy observation, but nevertheless it seems almost incredible that the Germans had no idea that a large scale-attack was about to begin.

The attack was planned to begin at a point where enemy forward troops were most vulnerable. Their recent advance of about 40 miles in places had left them with extended communications that severely stretched their logistical support. The spring offensives had cost them a great number of

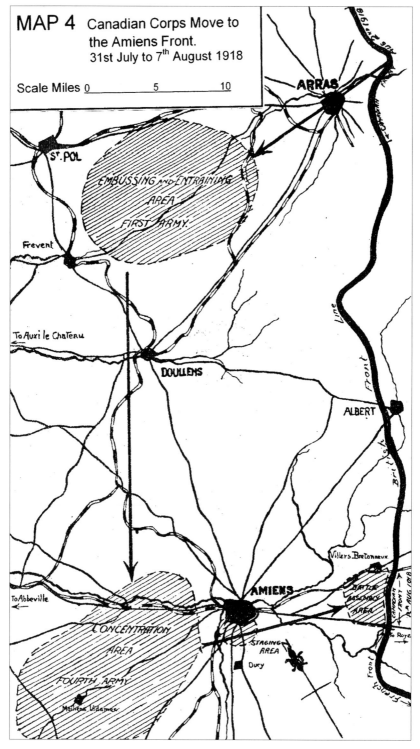

Canadian Corps' Move to the Amiens Front, 31 July to 7 August 1918.

casualties and morale was low, despite their apparent military success. In Germany, food was short and messages from home were not encouraging for their already undernourished troops.

Secrecy was further preserved by forbidding the artillery to carry out any preliminary shelling to register their targets before the battle began on 8 August. The CBSO had been able to prepare detailed maps of the location of the enemy batteries and make them available to the artillery. The training of the gunners and the careful calibration of the weapons enabled them to fire using these maps and hit targets accurately without prior registration.

With its propitious timing and location, the Allied counter attack was very successful, but the rapid advance could not be sustained and the enemy fell back on well-prepared defensive positions on the former battlefields around the Somme. General Currie's response to this setback was to suggest it should be turned to Allied advantage by switching the Canadian Corps back to their familiar surroundings not far from Arras. From there they would be able to mount an attack on the Hindenburg Line, leaving the enemy isolated in their salient where advances by French troops had been made in the battle on the River Marne further south. This judgement call by General Currie was supported by his superior officers, and turned out to be crucially effective.

------ooo------

Diaries for August 1918

ETRUN August/1. Fair weather.

CRA proceeds to VILLERS BRETTONNEUX Area to look over new area. Portion to be taken over by Canadian Corps is now being held by the French and will be taken over by the Australian Corps to-morrow.

Conference at 1st Can Division Hdqrs of GOs C Infantry Bde and CRA to discuss operation to be carried out to release AMIENS – PARIS Railways. 1st CDA Units on completion of relief march to HOUVIN Area.

ETRUN and in motor on roads in vicinity of AMIENS and PONT DE METZ. August/2. Rain.

Command of Field Artillery on the VITASSE, TELEGRAPH HILL and FEUCHY Section passes to CRAs 56th & 57th Divisions at 10.00am. CRA proceeds to AMIENS area by car to arrange about arrival of units of 1st CDA which entrain at FREVENT, PETIT HOUVIN and LIGNY and detrain PROUZEL, BACOUEL & NAMPS.

13 trains in all are used for transhipping of Div Arty. Much difficulty is experienced in obtaining information at detraining points partly owing to

the fact that these have been taken over from the French to-day. Weather remained very bad during entire day – and this combined with the fact that the two motor cycles accompanying CRA's car broke down in turn made our difficulties greater than was thought normal.

Temporary headquarters for the night were found at PONT DE METZ south of AMIENS. Arrangements were made by Can Corps Q to give 1st CDA Hdqrs in Chateau LONGUEAU from to-morrow.

Field guns are about to be used in close support of the infantry as they advance during the assault. Since gun barrels wear during sustained firing, it was most important that their condition and performance were assessed periodically. This had to be carried out in specially prepared ranges where measurements could be made of each gun's performance. Individual gun calibration charts could then be prepared.

All movements have to be planned to minimise the possibility of detection by the enemy. The cover of darkness is thus sought wherever possible.

PONT DE METZ/LONGUEAU August/3. Fair weather.

Trains began arriving at 6.30am and kept on at intervals thru out the day from three to six hours later.

18pdr batteries of 1st Bde are being sent during afternoon or night to VAUX-EN-AMIENOIS for calibration.

As no movement of transport is allowed before 9pm except what is absolutely essential, all units remain in vicinity of detraining points until dusk, moving to BOIS DE BOVES during the night.

Brigade Commanders and CRA visit prospective positions near CACHY, SW VILLERS, BRETTONEUX and change one location of 18pdr battery.

Wire received that 77th Army Brigade RFA is marching at 9.30pm from BELLOY SUR SOMME to BOVES wood. This brigade is one of the five brigades in the 1st CDA Group for the operation.

The 1st Canadian Divisional Artillery has been allocated a British Army artillery brigade to strengthen further artillery support for the Canadians during the initial assault.

LONGUEAU August/4. Dull.

Owing to congestion of traffic on roads during last night 77th Army Brigade were forced to go into temporary wagon lines between AMIENS and CAGNY in shelter of woods along river.

1st CDA units complete arrival at BOVES Wood about 8.30am. Congestion of troops in this wood is very bad. Watering facilities for horses is very poor.

In spite of strict orders against abnormal movement on roads forward, the movement on roads both forward and rear almost equals that during PASSCHENDAELE operation.

The concentration of forces in preparation for the assault led to congestion on the very limited number of roads. Furthermore, ammunition dumps were withdrawn far to the rear during the enemy advance, placing a great strain on the transport needed to bring up supplies in preparation for the planned Allied artillery bombardment.

Prospective battery positions in vicinity of CACHY are visited and battery commanders of 77th Army Bde RFA shown positions of 2nd Bde CFA which they will take over to-morrow morning.

First ammunition is taken forward – 200 rds per 18pdr and 150 rds per How [howitzer] will be attempted during the night. This will be one third of total to be taken up in three nights.

LONGUEAU August/5. Dull with rain at intervals.

Ammunition in battery positions is found well camouflaged at day break. Amount contemplated for last night was not quite reached. This was due to a combination of unforeseen difficulties which for to-night's supply will be overcome.

Four guns per battery will be taken forward and camouflaged to-night, remainder to-morrow night. Only skeleton crews who will also act as a guard will be forward before Y/Z night (7/8th August).

LONGEAU August/6. Fair with showers at intervals.

Abnormal movement on all roads continues, but as long as visibility remains as poor as it is to-day nothing will be given away to the enemy.

As yet enemy appears to be ignorant of the preparations, probably placing increased movement down to the fact that the Australians have recently relieved the French in this Sector.

The carefully concealed secret of the presence of the Canadian Corps in this sector is evidently intact. Vimy, Hill 70 and Passchendaele have made the Germans wary of them, and their knowledge of a Canadian presence would persuade them to prepare to resist a counter offensive. German experience of facing Canadian troops has always been traumatic.

1st Can Div Hdqrs is not coming forward until to-morrow afternoon. This arrangement increases the difficulties of those in the forward area as any matter of importance must be decided after consultation with Divisional Staff about twenty miles away.

Hdqrs 1st CDA is now minus a motor [car] owing to a break-down yesterday. New car has been demanded but will take several days at least to arrive. In the meantime CRA is without a car except for the time when one can be borrowed.

Communications continue to be problematic. The Canadian Corps will coordinate the barrages to be carried out as their infantry advances. Maps of these barrages and the timing of their 'lifts' must be planned by the CBSO at Corps level. Thus, it falls to 1st CDA HQ to receive the outlines from Corps HQ and translate them into detailed plans for the brigades under their command.

Barrage Maps for 18pdrs arrive early afternoon but 4.5 Howitzer Barrages are not arranged till late at night.

Enemy shelling of Forward Area is increasing due probably to great increase of movement over ground visual by ground observation to the enemy. No enemy balloons and practically no enemy aircraft are seen.

LONGUEAU/GENTELLES WOOD August/7. Fair.

Roads do not appear as congested as during the past few days. Advanced Hdqrs moves to dugouts at GENTELLES WOOD during afternoon.

Final preparations are made for the attack to-morrow. At the last hour it is found that 6" Newton ammunition will not be available. This is most unfortunate as 1st CDTM Bde were forward in Assembly positions before this was definitely known.

2nd Bde CFA moves to their Assembly area from positions at 12 midnight. Weather looks favorable for the attack.

8 August was the day Ludendorff called the blackest day for the German Army. Surprise was complete, partly because all previous preparations had been well concealed, but also because no registration of artillery targets were allowed. This meant that the barrages opened up using map references rather than the visually confirmed fall of shell fire. Therefore, it was necessary to establish the bearing from each gun and the relative altitude of the target above sea level. Range tables for each gun for standard conditions had been prepared. The actual conditions for each battery – wind speed and direction, temperature and barometric pressure – were provided from observations measured at divisional HQs. The state of technology at the time undoubtedly led to errors in these calculations, which all had to be made manually, and inevitably targets would not always hit by individual guns. Therefore, it was necessary for more than 900 guns to be employed by Allied artillery to smother enemy opposition.

The response of the enemy was only effective in a few areas, but even there it was quickly smothered by counter battery fire. The field artillery used shrapnel rather than high explosives so that the ground to be covered by the attacking tanks and cavalry would not be heavily cratered. Further ahead, smoke was employed both to confuse the enemy and to warn the infantry that heavy artillery was firing on targets beyond. However, the plan was to ensure that no heavy artillery fire would be brought down closer than 600 yards beyond the field artillery barrage. Mobile batteries of field artillery were moved forward so that they could be brought into action within 2,500 yards of the enemy front lines as the advance continued.

GENTELLES WOOD/STOVES WOOD V23b North of CAYEUX August/8.

Night passed very quietly. All Tanks and cavalry and mobile artillery units have first use of all main roads and bridges.

Barrage opened very well at 4.20am. In spite of the fact that there was no previous registration barrage was very regular and bursts effectively low.

2nd Brigade move forward over GENTELLES Ridge at Zero plus sixty. Nothing further is heard until a message which is broken off in the middle states that 2nd Bde CFA Hdqrs are established in V13 with 5th Battery CFA pulling into action between MORGEMONT WOOD and MARCEL CAVE at 7.45am.

At the end of the prearranged barrage (Zero plus four hours) 5th CDA and 77th Army Bde RFA form a group under CRA 5th CDN Division and pass to Can Corps Reserve. At this hour 1st Bde CFA move forward to reinforce 2nd Bde CFA in the captured territory – also 41st Brigade RGA (two 6" Howitzers and two 60pdr batteries all horse drawn) comes under control of CRA 1st Cdn Division.

Due to speed at which infantry advanced and to the constant change of infantry units (each Inf Bde passing thru another to the capture of a further objective) only elements of field artillery were in touch with advanced infantry posts until final objective was reached. All batteries were in position covering 1st Can Div Front on final objective at 4.30pm. Field Artillery NW of CAIX and E of CAYEUX. Heavy Artillery came to vicinity of IGNACOURT and CAYEUX during evening.

Personnel of 1st CDTM Bde during day proceeded with advancing infantry outposts (in many cases in front of them) and turned enemy guns on retreating enemy. About 500 rds were fired at enemy during the day.

Hdqrs 1st CDA move forward with Divisional Hdqrs to huts in STOVES WOOD V13b North of CATEUX.

Flanking Divisions appear to have gained practically all objectives although 3rd Can Div on right had more resistance to overcome than 1st

A 60-pdr being hitched with horses through a village. (*Courtesy of the RCA Museum*)

or 2nd Can Divisions. Casualties in artillery were a few horses and OPs wounded by m.g. fire.

The infantry brigades were able to move forward meeting little organised resistance, leapfrogging each other to bring fresh troops into action with each surge of advance.

The Canadians captured 161 enemy guns on the first day of the offensive. Of these, twenty-six were brought into action afterwards, firing a total of 1,500 rounds at their former owners. Technical information was already available, including range tables for each piece. Furthermore, captured copies of maps showing the locations of all hostile batteries in the area were invaluable for further confirming the work of the CBSO.

In the first day of the offensive, the infantry front line moved ahead 8 miles.

STOVES WOOD August/9. Day opened well – low cloud with prospects of local showers.

Orders received in early morning that Can Corps would continue the advance with same order of battle as on previous day, but objectives farther south which necessitates a side slipping to the right before Zero Hour.

Objectives are ROUVROY – MENARICOURT. During early morning 4th Can Div cleared up situation which was rather obscure at LE QUESNOY EN SANTERRE.

Advance began at 1pm with 1st Can Inf Bde on right covered by 1st Bde CFA and 2nd Can Inf Bde on left covered by 2nd Bde CFA. Each Artillery brigade acted under orders of GOsC Inf Bdes covered thru out the day. This arrangement seemed to produce very good results although it is thought that more "open sight" work with forward single guns might inspire greater morale in our attacking forces. This new method will be given a trial on the next days advance.

Very gallant bit of work was done by a section of 4th Battery CFA under MAJOR A O McMURTRY on m.g. nests in vicinity of BEAUFORT. This officer again cleared up a difficult situation S of ROUVROY later in the day. Lieut DAWSON 1st Bde CFA in charge of artillery patrol did particularly good work – borne out by statement of GOC 1st Can Inf Bde.

All objectives for the day were gained by 1st Can Division: Contact was established with Inf of flanking Divisions soon after final objectives were reached. Whole Divisional Front was well covered by Field Artillery barrage for SOS purposes during the night. An Arty Bde (41st) continued thru out the night to harass enemy roads and probable assembly points in vicinity of BEAUFORT.

Warning Order received the advance will be continued to-morrow by 4th Can Division on the left and 32nd Division (Imperial) on right. Objectives will be ROYE – HATTENCOURT – HALLU joining up with Australians at railway S. of CHAULNES.

The allied advance continues, but enemy resistance is stiffening. The Canadian infantry front line has moved forward 3 miles during the second day.

STOVES WOOD/BEAUFORT August/10. Fair weather.

4th Canadian Div & 32nd Div are to "Jump Off" at 8am but do not get started until 10.30am. Role of 1st Can Division with 1st CDA, 77th Army Bde and 41st Bde RGA will be to make preparations along the line of final objective of yesterday to resist probable counter attack. Batteries are being sited with this end in view.

HQs 1st CDA and 1st CDN Division move to BEAUFORT CHATEAU K5c.

4th Can Div advance on left to objectives detailed but owing to hold up of right Division attached to Can Corps at PARVILLERS 4th Can Div have to evacuate some of captured ground on right. Right Division is held up practically on Jumping Off line.

Enemy bombing at night is very heavy causing a few casualties among horses of other divisions of the Corps.

The enemy is beginning to fall back on well-defended trench systems and the advance during the third day is only around 2 miles. 1st CDA HQ has moved up to be within 3½ miles of the front line. GHQ is clearly wishing to take the initiative to resume the offensive and issues orders to this effect.

BEAUFORT August/11. Visibility very good.

Very difficult task presented itself in yesterdays operations. The objective for the day was beyond a very strongly organized system of Trench viz. The German Front and support line System which was held previous to 1916 Somme Offensive. The wire was still intact and trenches in fair condition. Needless to say the Hun with m.g.s every two yards (as prisoner stated) had an easy time repelling isolated attempts of our patrols to break thru. This system will require an organized assault with a Creeping Barrage and organized Counter Battery Work.

4th Can Division is driven in from occupation of HALLU S of CHAULNES by strong enemy counter attack. 32nd Divisional Sector is more or less obscure. Apparently the enemy has held up everything very solidly by retaining his hold on PARVILLERS and DAMERY. Bombing activity over [our] rear areas very pronounced – amount of damage is however very small compared with what should result from the number of bombs dropped on a starry night.

Far from being able to take the initiative, the Canadian infantry has been unable to hold some of their gains of the previous day. The great advances of the first week having come to an end, it is clear that the plans for further attacks on this front must be carefully considered.

BEAUFORT August/12. Fine weather continues.

Outpost line remains practically as it was yesterday. Situation between FOUQUESCOURT and PARVILLERS remains obscure but towards evening when 3rd Can Div takes over from 32nd Division a definite line is established which shows 4th Can Div in possession of FOUQUESCOURT but with outpost line of 3rd Can Div in touch with support line of 4th Can Div. BLACK WOOD SW FOUQUESCOURT still remains in hands of enemy. This forms a very serious re-entrant in our line as it is practically in rear of 44th Battn in FOUQUESCOURT.

Warning Order given from RA Can Corps that a very large operation involving a Creeping Barrage and an organized assault in general will take place on 15th August by Can Corps in conjunction with Australian Corps on left and XXXI French Corp on right. From 4pm – 8pm impression was that 1st and 2nd Can Divisions would operate from right to left. This was changed however and 3rd Can Div will attack on right instead of 1st Can Division.

Four times during the day orders were changed, regarding operations during the course of the next few days. For several hours it was believed that 1st Can Division would operate on the sector FRAMERVILLE – LIHONS allowing the Australian Corps to contract. (Australian Corps has been engaged in minor operations during the whole summer.)

Bombing activity at night continues. Enemy aircraft have strengthened considerably since 8th August due probably to adoption of our tactics viz rushing many of best airmen to scene of operations.

GHQ is undecided on how to proceed. Despite issuing orders for the artillery to prepare the ground for a further advance, there is some doubt whether or not this could be successful. Enemy defences in this area are very strong. They had developed some excellent defensive systems in the earlier Somme battlefields.

BEAUFORT August/13. Weather continues very fine. Dust on roads is very bad.

Conference of CRAs of 1st, 3rd and 5th Canadian Divisions & CRA 32nd Division is held at UMBRELLA APPLE TREE east of FOLIES at 9am to discuss disposition of artillery for the coming operation. Order from right to left will be 32nd DA, 1st CDA, Ralston's Group, 5th CDA. Battery positions must be within 2000 yards of our own Front Line. 1st CDA area is in vicinity of LE QUESNOY. As "Z" day is stated to be 15th (anniversary of HILL 70 operation). Guns & ammunition are being taken forward to-night.

Area is very much exposed but fortunately is cut up well with trenches in which guns and ammunition can be hidden without much work. Enemy artillery activity is noticeably increasing. Apparently quite a number of batteries has reinforced this front. LE QUESNOY area which particularly interests this Div Arty at present received several "area-strafes" during the afternoon and evening. BOUCHOIR, where forward Ammunition Dump is being established to-day has been heavily shelled with 5.9s [enemy artillery].

It is questionable whether this attack will be carried out. The enemy now has had sufficient time to reinforce the Line Troops and as the element of surprise from our point of view has been eliminated it is doubtful whether it really will be undertaken. Sound Ranging Sections [now an established electronic method of detecting enemy artillery] are only to-night starting to work on location of his batteries and as it has taken at least two or three days to get first locations properly, it is thought the operation will hardly be attempted before PARVILLERS which is still holding out.

CAPT ROBINSON, 2nd How Bty CFA is reported wounded during night. This makes a very great shortage of senior officers in this brigade as only four now remain effective.

BEAUFORT August/14. Fine weather – hot and dusty.

Two guns per battery and more than half requested amount of ammunition is taken to positions in LE QUESNOY area. Practically no casualties result. One gun of 6th Bty CFA receives direct hit during "area-strafe" at LE QUESNOY.

About 6.30pm word is received from 1st Can Div "G" that the operation is or will be postponed more or less indefinitely. In view of this all further preparations are stopped until further orders. Coupled with this message is a warning that 1st Can Div will relieve 3rd Can Division commencing 15/16th.

Bombs are dropped quite close to HQs 1st CDA during the early night.

BEAUFORT August/15. Fine weather but roads and country very dusty.

More casualties resulted in getting gun of 6th Battery out of position in LE QUESNOY area. If much night activity is necessitated in this Battle position area, our casualties will quickly rise up in numbers.

Inf relief in 1st and 3rd Cdn Div Relief commences to-night. Command passes from GOC 3rd Can Div to GOC 1st Can Div at 12 noon to-morrow.

3rd Can Div Arty will be withdrawn to wagon lines to-night and to-morrow thereafter proceeding to rear areas.

Policy laid down for artillery action until further orders is to make the enemy think we are going to continue the attack and at the same time make preparations to repel an enemy counter attack in strength.

BEAUFORT/LE QUESNEL August/16. Fair weather during day, cloudy towards night.

HQs 1st CDA moves to Chateau at LE QUESNEL at 12 noon. During the day offices will be in Chateau building. During the night offices will be in caves in close proximity. On arrival at LE QUESNEL, find everything in state of excitement. French on right report enemy is retiring. Orders are issued to 2nd and 3rd Can Inf Bdes that they must press forward taking advantage of any retirement but on no account to engage in battle. 2nd C I Bde which normally would not relieve until night go forward at once to go thru 9th C I Bde in the line.

New policy for artillery support is being tried (Detailed in Arty Instr. 35(3)). All artillery units (mobile) are in touch with respective Inf Bdes by 2.30pm. By night not much progress has been made. 3rd C I Bde push forward on both sides of LA CHAVATTE, taking SCHWETZ Wood about 6pm.

Lack of great progress is due to strict orders regarding "not to engage in battle". French on right are making organized attacks during the afternoon. GOYENCOURT is captured by the French.

4.00pm. Infantry are held up temporarily in front of LA CHAVATTE. Situation is reported well in hand. Artillery will be notified when fire is required. Rearmost batteries of 5th CDA are moving forward to positions S of ROUVROY. Reconnaissance is being made of new battery positions in vicinity of PARVILLERS.

4.27pm. 41st Bde RGA and 98th Double Heavy Group are ordered to commence slow bombardment of LA CHEVATTE. Fire will stop at 4.53pm. Field artillery is now engaging Trenches immediately W of LA CHEVATTE.

4.40pm. Right Inf Bde bombing up Trenches from SW towards FRESNOY. BLAVET Wood is now well in possession.

5.00pm. 1st Bde CFA (2nd C I Bde mobile Arty Bde) is assembled at UMBRELLA TREE East of FOLIES. One battery has gone forward about an hour ago under orders of OC 10th C Battn. 2nd Bde CFA (3rd C I Bde mobile Arty Bde) is assembled immediately East of BOUCHOIR. Two sections are under orders to go forward: one with 13th C I Battn and other with 16th Can I Battn.

5.05pm. French Liaison Officer reports enemy concentrating for Counter ATTACK in BOIS de CROISETTE and Bois de BRAQUEMONT about 4.15pm but that owing to Heavy Concentration by our Heavy Artillery opening at this time all signs of Counter Attack died quickly.

5.10pm. 2nd Bde CFA reported assembling between PARVILLERS and LE QUESNOY. One section only proceeded forward – this with 16th Battn. Good work (reported by OC 16th Battn to GOC 3rd C I Bde) done by this section on LA CHAVATTE.

6.15pm. 150th A Bde CFA is moving forward to positions E of LE QUESNOY. 14th Bde CFA now in position South of ROUVROY.

Altho there was no real test made of mobile artillery arrangements as laid down in Arty Instr 35(3), GOsC Inf Bdes seem to think from to-days work that arrangements would be very satisfactory. Personal touch between Mobile Artillery Commanders and Inf GOsC appears to be the only liaison method which gives good results. This has proved itself in battle on 8th, 9th and 10th and also to-day.

The C W Wireless as a means of communication between mobile artillery units and Arty Hdqrs has shown itself to be the only one dependable for open warfare. These sets can be put into action within 15 minutes and therefore send back location of artillery units and special information within 30 minutes of taking up a new position.

LE QUESNOY August/17. Cloudy weather during most of day. Flies and [bad] water are producing a great number of cases of dysentery in the 1st Can Div.

5.00am. In order to assist the French in an organized attack on ROYE which began at 4.30am, 41st, 98th & 40th Heavy Artillery Brigades and over 1 brigade Field Artillery of 32nd DA Group place a concentration on area about BOIS de l'ABBÉ north of ROYE from 5.00 – 5.15am.

8.50am. French again request assistance. Concentrated shoot by Heavies and Field will take place from 9.00 – 9.30am on southern outskirts of FRESNOY. French report they are being held up by m.g. fire all along Front of attack.

9.00am. 3rd C I Bde report capture of LA CHAVATTE in early morning without much opposition.

The general policy remains in force: "Not to engage in battle but to press forward patrols wherever possible to take advantage of any retirement or weakness in the enemy".

Slow bombardment from 3.00pm to 8.45pm of SALMON and OBERNON Trenches and FRESNOY. This will be followed by 5 minute burst of shrapnel by Field Artillery over whole area bombarded. The general idea was that if the enemy were thinking of retiring this would give him an added incentive to quicken his movement and allow our infantry to occupy these trenches and also town of FRESNOY.

About 9.30pm both infantry brigades report enemy was still holding SALMON and OBERNON Trenches and FRESNOY. This means that our outpost line will remain where it was during the day.

French are rather expecting a counter attack from NE during the night. They now have a flank more or less exposed from NE part of GOYENCOURT to GARE de ROYE. Enemy appears to be wishing to fight every backward step at present moment. This of course may only be covering his preparations for retirement beyond the SOMME.

LE QUESNEL August/18. Cloudy with few scattered showers in early morning but otherwise fair.

32nd Div Arty withdraw to wagon lines during the night leaving only six brigades of Field Artillery covering the 1st Can Div Front. 32nd DA are marching during the day to Australian Corps area on the left.

Definite jumping-off line is given for next operation which will take place about 23rd inst. Field Arty positions for 8 brigades are being chosen this afternoon not farther west than line: Western Edge FOUQUESCOURT – Western Edge PARVILLERS – BOIS EN Z. Preparations for Resection and dumping ammunition are being made with all possible speed.

During the day HAG cut wire on SALMON and OBERNON Trenches along the lines laid down by 3rd Can Div on 15th inst.

French are making series of attacks east of GOYENCOURT during afternoon and evening. Our Heavies and Field gives assistance several times during afternoon and night.

7.00pm. Warning order received that Can Corps will be relieved very shortly. Rumor states that it will be by the French.

This is the first time that information is received at divisional level about the plans being made to move the Canadian Corps to engage the enemy further north. However, details are being withheld because of the need for secrecy. Map 5 shows details of the advances made by the Canadian Corps from 8 to 17 August.

Ammunition situation in view of French relief is serious. Our 60,000rds of 18pdr ammunition is lying about the forward area. This should be solved before relief is complete.

Hurried preparations are being made to collect all captured guns to gun park at LONGUEAU within the next 36 hours.

150th and 179th Arty Brigades RFA withdraw to wagon lines after 10pm. Only four FA Bdes are now left covering the Front. 1st and 2nd Bdes CFA covering 2nd Can Inf Bde in right subsector: 13th and 14th Bdes CFA covering 3rd Can Inf Bde in left subsector.

LE QUESNEL August/19. Fine weather.

Representatives from 126th French Division visit headquarters to arrange relief. French artillery will take new positions and at 8am 21st August assume responsibility for the Front.

French on right request more artillery assistance to ward off probable counter attacks – this takes the form of five minute bursts from Heavies and Field Artillery from 10am to 1pm. Nothing developed during the course of the day.

1st Cdn Divisional Infantry are being relieved on nights 19/20, 20/21st and 21/22nd August.

Rumor reports 2nd Cdn Div marching north with 3rd Can Div following at 24 hours.

Ammunition in all battery positions scattered over the forward area is being collected to BOUCHOIR and LE QUESNEL Dumps. RA Can Corps has volunteered the services of ten lorries for this task to report to DEMUIN at 8pm to-night. Captured guns are being rapidly cleared to LONGUEAU Gun Park.

1st Cdn Div Front remains fairly quiet. Hostile artillery activity decreasing but appears to be increasing on our immediate right probably due to persistency of French patrol in pressing the enemy with minor attacks daily. Enemy still holds ST MARD and ROYE station.

LE QUESNEL August/20. Fine weather, very sultry in afternoon.

Representatives from French Corps on right overrun 1st Cdn Div HQs during the morning spreading enthusiasm in their wake. An attack by three French Corps will take place at 2pm. Our Heavies and Field are co-operating with heavy bombardment from 8am to 2.15pm on FRESNOY, BOIS DE

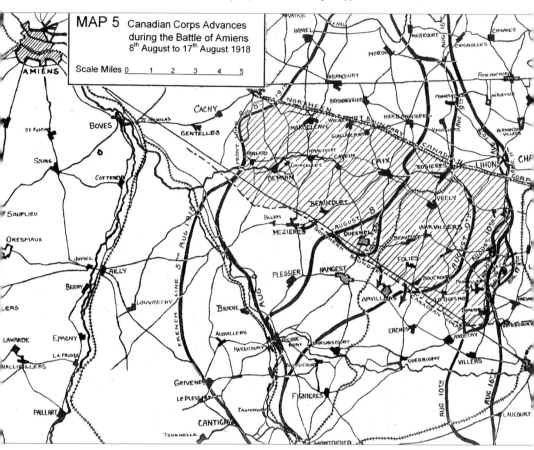

Canadian Corps' Advances during the Battle of Amiens.

CROISSETTE, BOIS de l'ABBAYE and GRUNY. Altho none of these are within French objectives, bombardment is desired with a view to keeping down hostile machine gun fire.

If enthusiasm can help materially to win a battle then ROYE will be taken easily to-day.

5.00pm. Requests from French for artillery fire on BOIS de l'ABBAYE as counter attack is expected. No definite news about what advance was made during the afternoon.

1st Cdn Div Front fairly quiet during the day.

Ammunition is being rapidly cleared up in forward area. This is being assisted considerably by increased expenditure during the day.

No bombing in LE QUESNEL area in spite of very bright moonlight.

Although German forces had not been routed, the confidence of their commanders, particularly General Ludendorff, had been severely affected.

The Canadian Corps, under General Currie, had nevertheless achieved a great victory. Over 9,000 prisoners, 190 guns and 1,000 machine guns and trench mortars had been taken in the course of the battle. But German resistance was stiffening after an initial near-collapse. Currie advised that the Canadian Corps should now move north again to spearhead the assault on the strongly fortified Hindenburg Line. His advice was accepted and another secret move was undertaken. The French on their right and the Australians on their left would take over their front.

Detail taken from picture on p. 63. (*Courtesy of the RCA Museum*)

CHAPTER FIVE

Overcoming the German Defences on The Hindenburg Line

The Battle of Arras, 21 August – 3 September 1918

The Canadian Corps was now to undertake their most significant battles of the war. The enemy had constructed a formidable line of defence in the French and Belgian territories taken during the winter months of 1914 – the famous Hindenburg Line. Using the best military techniques available at the time, the Germans had designed a series of obstacles to defeat any attacker. Beginning with the old German front system east of Monchy-le-Preux and the Fresney–Rouvroy Line, a multi-layered arrangement of mutually defended trenches and strong points had been established. The most important of these was the Drocourt–Queant Line. The Vis-en-Artois Switch on this line had to be overcome to create the opportunity to drive the enemy back from the most strongly held parts of the Hindenburg Line in a series of set-piece assaults.

The movement of the Canadian Corps to the Arras area was carried out progressively as they were relieved of their responsibilities on the Amiens Front. 1st CDA remained to support the troops taking over the Amiens Front from the Canadians.

Plans for these operations were well advanced; 1st CDA, having had to be the last in the Canadian Corps to disengage from their role near Amiens, were to go into action very rapidly after their arrival at the new battle front. The rail journey had been subject to many delays but the initial attacks in preparation for the assaults on the Hindenburg Line had to go ahead as planned. The first attacks were fiercely resisted by the enemy, but the breakthrough was sustained by the infantry, closely supported by their artillery. The breaking of the Vis-en-Artois Switch, the strongest part of the enemy defence system at this point, was the key to the Allies' subsequent success.

Having lost the Vis-en-Artois Switch, the Germans retired reluctantly to their next line of defence, the Canal du Nord. But before the Canadians could face this next challenge, they needed time to recover after the bloody fight for the Vis-en-Artois Switch. Replacement of men lost and work on the maintenance of their equipment was essential; the Canadians had been working under battlefield conditions since the beginning of August.

------ooo------

Diaries for 21 August Onwards

The Canadian Corps 2nd and 4th Divisions were the first to reach their new front south of Arras. Meanwhile, the 1st, 3rd and 5th Divisional Artilleries remained near Roye until their positions had been handed over to the French and the bombardments they had requested in their support during the handover had been completed.

LE QUESNEL August/21. Fair weather.

Command of artillery passed to French Artillery Commandant, 126 Division at 8am. French are now holding Right Brigade Subsection. As 3rd Can Inf Bde still remains in left subsection, 5th CDA still remain in action until direct touch is got with French artillery which were supposed to be in action and in touch with all line infantry by 8am.

Reports are received of a British attack early this morning on 3rd Army Front. Good progress is reported by 9am – COURCELLES, ACHIET LE PETIT and BEAUMONT SUR ANCRE reported as captured.

1st and 5th Can Div Artys withdraw to wagon lines at 8.30pm. 1st CDA marches by night to CAYEUX area. 5th CDA marches by night under orders of 1st Can Div Arty to rear area.

Sub Staff 1st CDA HQs moves to CAGNY/ (SE of AMIENS during evening by lorries which have completed collecting 18pdr ammunition in LE QUESNOY area and are proceeding back to Lorry Park.

LE QUESNEL/CAGNY August/22. Fair and very warm.

HQs 1st CDA move during morning to Chateau in CAGNY about two miles SE of AMIENS on road to BOVES.

All units 1st CDA visited on road from LE QUESNEL to CAGNY. Everyone very comfortable and in good spirits.

Gun Park of captured guns visited at LONGUEAU. All Canadian captures and some Australian captures were parked in this place. All calibres were represented 4.2, 5.9 & 8" Howitzers; 7.7, 4.2 guns; 7.7, 4.2 & 5.9 HV Guns; Anti Aircraft guns of all descriptions; Trench Mortar (light and medium);

and m.g.s both light and heavy in hundreds. The whole presented a very imposing array and shows in a slight degree the extent of the blow dealt the Hun on and after the 8th August.

Australian Corps administer all Canadians left in this area from noon to-day.

The 1st CDA are handing over their responsibilities on this front to the French. It is still unclear where they are to go but they have had enough information to know that they must collect all their ammunition in preparation for a major move. In fact they are to return to their familiar ground near Arras where many of their successful actions in 1917 had taken place. There, they are to form the spearhead of the forces attacking the Hindenburg Line, a very strongly prepared defensive system held in great depth by the enemy.

Orders for march of 1st CDA Units do not arrive till 5.30pm. All branches of 1st Can Div must march along VALLEY ROAD to-night. As no stated hour is given for individual units to move off, all artillery are ordered to move at 8.30pm or as soon after as can be arranged with[out] interfering with other arty units. Two brigades move to vicinity of DOMART: 1st CDAC and 1st CDTM Bde to HANGARD. An exceptionally bright moonlight night for the march.

CAGNY August/23. Fair weather continues with very dusty roads.

Congestion of traffic occurred on VALLEY ROAD last night as was expected. Artillery units appeared not to suffer to any extent owing to heads of units being established on roads by 8.30pm. All moves were completed by 2am.

Orders for further move to BOVES WOOD area to-night. No moves will be ordered until 12 midnight as many 1st Cdn Div units are in GENTELLES WOOD area and will block all movement until they are cleared.

Attack in direction of CHAULIVES is reported to have been made by Australians at dawn this morning. Satisfactory progress is reported at 11am.

Apparently camouflage of movement is being tried again. 2nd & 3rd Cdn Divisions are reported to be now in the line at ARRAS. Detraining points for 1st CDA are too far north to make believe all Canadians are proceeding to ARRAS area.

1st CDA are apparently the last to move away from the Amiens Front. It has been an exceptionally successful campaign and General Currie has been informally congratulated by his former Corps Commander (during the Vimy Campaign) General Byng saying that this operation (the Battle of Amiens) by the Canadians was, in his opinion, the finest of the war. The penetrations made by the allied armies from 8 to 17 August and the location of the new spearhead south of Arras are shown in Map 6.

CAGNY August/24. Generally fair but with occasional showers.

Move of 1st CDA units completed by 4.30am. Billets at present in BOVES area in fair shape but if rain were to set in conditions would soon change for the worse.

RA Can Corps orders received regarding an attack to be made by 2nd and 3rd Cdn Div on ARRAS Front on 25th or 26th August. It will be similar to that of the 8th August on HANGARD. 1st Cdn Div will probably be used for exploitation on 2nd or 3rd day – sooner than this will not be practicable as artillery do not complete entraining until early morning 27th.

The general situation along the Front appears very satisfactory. We are engaging the Hun at almost all points along the Front – keeping him in such a state of expectancy that he doesn't quite know what will happen next. It is rumored that BAPAUME and NOYON have both fallen.

The French forces on the Marne have also achieved successes on their front. Their attacks will have further confused the Germans, who are struggling with the logistical problems arising from advancing so far and so fast since 21 March. Coping with Allied successes in several parts of the Western Front is placing a great strain on them; they have suffered heavy casualties and have moved many of their reserves south to resist the advances made against them on the Amiens Front. The change in Allied tactics to strike at the Hindenburg Line will soon necessitate withdrawals from the Somme area, which they had been preparing to defend strongly.

CAGNY August/25. Fair weather with thunder storms during the evening.

Units remain at BOVES WOOD until to-night when they move to their respective entraining points.

Visited RA Can Corps at NOYELLE VION and get details of contemplated attack. Role of 1st Cdn Div will be exploitation later on.

HQs 1st Cdn Div move during day to HERMAVILLE. This will only be temporary HQs for one day. Move to ETRUN expected later.

CAGNY/BERLES August/26. After night of thunder storms, morning opens quite fair.

Move to entraining points is made without mishap. All train departures are postponed three hours due to a wreck of some description on the line. 1st train will not probably leave until 3 or 4pm.

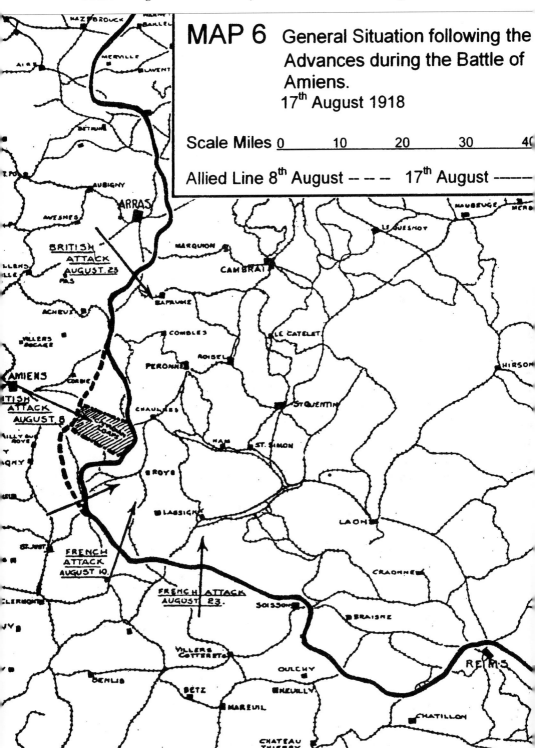

General Situation Following the Advances during the Battle of Amiens.

RA Can Corps visited about 6pm. Reports are very favorable of the attack. MONCHY was captured before 9am. 1st CDA are expected to join in action on 28th. This will scarcely be practicable owing to trains. As events are turning out it is very unfortunate that move was not made by road. All 1st CDA would have reached the ARRAS area by 25th August by easy staging. Probably now everything will be rushed forward from detraining points at last possible moment to cover 1st Cdn Div Infantry if in action on 28th inst.

HQs 1st CDA is established at BERLES Chateau for the night.

BERLES/ARRAS August/27. Cloudy turning to light rain towards late afternoon.

Artillery trains are all about eleven hours late in arriving. Journey which was scheduled to take five hours was ten hours for shortest trip. All units arriving before noon bivouac in vicinity of detraining points.

Orders are issued during morning for a march to vicinity of AINVILLE and WAGONLIEU in ARRAS area. This move is completed by all units before dark.

So much for secrecy! The delays caused by the train journey have made it necessary to press on with all speed if the 1st CDA is to be in position to support their infantry's initial assault.

According to latest orders 1st Cdn Div will relieve 2nd Cdn Div on right of Cdn Corps on night of 28th/29th August. 2nd CDA HQs visited but owing to all HQs being on the move not much information on which a relieving unit could act was obtainable. Task of this division will be the capture of QUEANT – DROCOURT line immediately south of ARRAS – CAMBRAI road providing it has not been taken prior to night 28th/29th. Amount of artillery will probably be Field – 7 brigades, Heavy – 3 brigades. The operation at present appears to be one requiring Corps coordination as the enemy line of resistance is well organized and very strong along whole Corps front. 4.5 How Smoke is being demanded to screen approach of Tanks to this QUEANT – DROCOURT line of Trenches.

One of the great advantages of the Canadian Corp having four divisions acting together was that all their artillery resources could be concentrated to support their infantry during assaults on key objectives.

Orders are issued to brigades & DAC to move to BEAURAINS – TELEGRAPH HILL – NEUVILLE VITASSE Area before 10am to-morrow 28th August. It is expected that 1st & 2nd Bdes will move into action near CHERISY on night 28/29th August.

Considerable HV Gun [enemy] fire on roads in Forward Area and on ARRAS.

ARRAS/NEUVILLE VITASSE August/28. Rain at intervals thru out the day.

1st and 2nd Brigades CFA and 1st CDAC move to BEAURAINS Area during morning. Warning is given to be prepared to move during early evening into action in vicinity of CHERISY.

HQs 2nd CDA visited in NEUVILLE VITASSE area. 2nd Can Div are engaged to-day in an attack on Trench System West if QUEANT – DROCOURT LINE. Atho 1st Objective was taken very quickly after the Jump Off it was not held. Final position for night was practically the same as during the morning before the attack. Divisions on either flank have pressed ahead during the day and leave this portion of Front as reentrant on our line.

HQs 1st CDA move to vicinity of present HQs 2nd CDA and prepare to relieve at midnight.

1st & 2nd Bdes CFA move forward during the afternoon and go into action under orders of 2nd CDA covering Right Inf Bde Front.

Communication to all units is at present very bad.

Ammunition supply is in very serious state owing to none reaching the Gun Area since yesterday morning. Lorries are on the road since early afternoon. Owing to traffic congestion it is difficult to say when they will arrive.

NEUVILLE VITASSE August/29. Fair weather. Slightly cooler than usual.

Artillery arrangements for covering the Front remain as when taken over at midnight until 2pm when original group boundaries were slightly altered. Grouping remains Right, Centre & Left with Right Group composed of 1st & 2nd CDAs with 282nd Army Bde RFA: Centre Group of 39th Div Arty: Left Group of 15th Div Arty.

An attack to establish a Jumping Off Line for QUEANT – DROCOURT Line will take place at dawn. This will be made by 1st Can Inf Bde. Attack will be made from the South along ULSTER & UNICORN Trenches and also along ORIX & OPAL Trenches from West. Barrage charts are late in reaching batteries owing to delay in obtaining detail. It will be due to exceptionally good work of the Battery Commanders that this operation is a success.

NEUVILLE VITASSE August/30. Cloudy but clearing to fair weather about noon.

Barrage this morning was a decided success. The effect was of two barrages at right angles joining and continuing in lifts to a final protective barrage. This caused confusion amongst the enemy who seemed anxious to

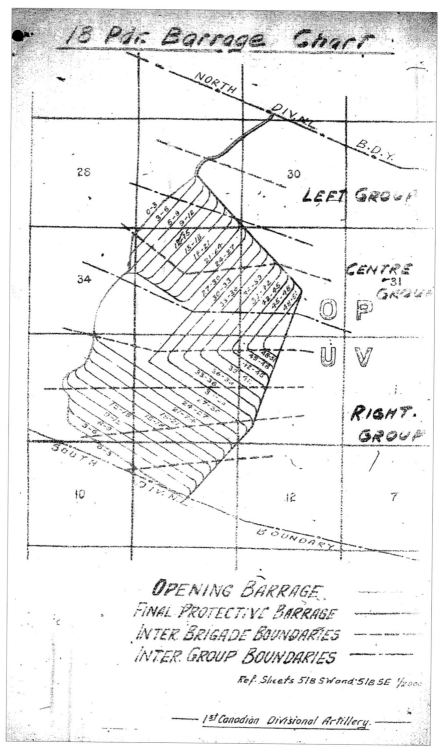

Ingenious barrages on the Fresney–Rouvroy line, 30 August 1918.

get out of 18pdr and 4.5" How barrages working in different directions at the same time. Considerable number of prisoners resulted. UPTON WOOD and UNION and UNICORN Trenches were easily captured. Enemy still held possession of OLIVE and OSTRICH Trenches and a fort called OCEAN WORK. These held out for the course of the day resisting all attempts to take it by 1st Can Inf Bde including one organized attempt with smoke and HE placed across the trenches north of OCEAN WORK.

The barrage carried out by the 1st CDA has been described in several reports about this battle. The plans for this barrage show that the training of the artillery brigades has given the artillery staff confidence that such complexity is well within their grasp. It proves to be a notable contribution to the preparations for the destruction of the Hindenburg Line. This action is a further confirmation of the technical and tactical ability of the Canadian gunners and their close liaison with the infantry under the most trying of battlefield conditions.

Counter attack during the afternoon caused an uncertain situation for several hours in vicinity of UPTON WOOD. Situation was restored during the early evening.

1st Can Division is still a considerable distance from J.O. line laid down for attack of QUEANT – DROCOURT Line. 2nd Can Inf Bde is given task of clearing up OCEAN WORK, OLIVE & OSTRICH Trenches to-night or at dawn to-morrow.

Situation on flanks is fluctuating. 57 Division on right is now reported to have lost HENDECOURT and RIENCOURT. 4th British Division on left is now reported west of HAUCOURT altho ST SERVINS Line has been in our possession at intervals during the day. It is most necessary that this latter place be held as it commands the area in which batteries must take up position to cover QUEANT – DROCOURT Line.

Points for wire cutting are given in the QUEANT – DROCOURT Line but as 4.5" Hows are not within wire cutting range the task must be carried out by Double Heavy Group.

NEUVILLE VITASSE August/31. Cloudy with rain. Fair in afternoon and evening.

Minor operation carried out at dawn by 2nd Can Inf Bde and supported by 39th and 15th Divisional Artilleries resulted in capture of OCEAN WORK, OLIVE and OSTRICH Trenches. Outposts were pushed out almost to Jumping Off Line in the valley north of ORIX Trench. ORIX and OPAL Trenches become ours to within 700 yards of Jumping Off Line.

Situation to the south will have to be cleared up to-night or at dawn to-morrow. Conference is held between GOsC 57th Division and 1st Can Div with a view to drawing up a Creeping Barrage for capture of CROWS NEST and CHATEAU WOOD north of HENDECOURT by 1st Can Div and of HENDECOURT by 57th Div.

At the last moment 2nd Can Inf Bde decide to push out to Jumping Off Line on its front East of UPTON WOOD. This operation extends to left and 12th Can Inf Bde will push out from CAMBRAI Road South.

4th Can Division take over north portion of 1st Can Div Front and south portion of 4th British Division Front tonight. 15th Div Arty passes to 4th Can Div at 8am to-morrow. For the operation in the morning 1st CDA is covering minor attacks by 3rd C I Bde, 2nd C I Bde and 12th C I Bde.

Diaries for September 1918

In order to set up the Jumping Off Line for the assault on the Drocourt–Queant Line, it was necessary to break the enemy defences a mile and a half in front of it. These consisted of the Fresney–Rouvroy Line and the strongly fortified defence system of Ocean Work and Upton Wood astride the Vis-en-Artois Switch. This switch system was a defensive line running to the rear that facilitated flanking attacks on troops that had broken through on either side of it. Breaking the hinge of this switch system where it joined the front line was critical to the success of this battle. 1st CDA succeeded in assisting the infantry to take these important positions.

NEUVILLE VITASSE September/1. Rain in early morning but clearing to fine weather about 9am.

All operations this morning commencing at 4.50am resulted in success: The outpost line being pushed forward almost to the Jumping Off Line. CROWS NEST, CHATEAU Wood and HENDECOURT were taken. Counter Attack about noon broke down quickly and situation restored.

Situation on right is to be bettered at 6.05pm. 57th Division is attacking RIENCOURT and will establish a Jumping Off Line East of this village. 63rd (Naval) Division will continue the attack on Front of Div on right after 57th Division has broken QUEANT DROCOURT Line in to-morrow's operation.

About dusk enemy made several attempts on ORIX and OPAL Trenches East of UPTON WOOD but all without success. Jumping Off Line as laid down previously was held during the evening and night.

Batteries have undergone a very strenuous time during the time since coming to this area. Practically each morning an attack of some description was made. This necessitated about 400 rds per gun being taken forward each night to positions which were usually well forward – in some cases under enemy m.g. fire.

Despite the savage but unsuccessful counter attacks made by the enemy to drive the Canadian infantry back from the positions they had occupied the previous day, the preparations for the main assault were completed. The assault on the Drocourt–Queant Line, that formed the northern extension of the Hindenburg Line, could now be undertaken as planned.

NEUVILLE VITASSE September/2. Weather fair with occasional showers.

Zero Hour for attack on QUEANT – DROCOURT Line is 5am. Previous to this hour the front remained fairly normal after the liveliness of early evening yesterday. Information thru out the attack was rather slow in getting back to Artillery HQs. RED LINE (1st Objective) was reached on scheduled time but onward from this line advance was slow.

3rd Can Inf Bde went forward strong and captured CAGNICOURT but were held up by heavy m.g. fire from south when attempting to go beyond: BOIS DE LOISON and BOIS DE BOUCHE were taken after the heights were taken on by Heavy Artillery: Advance beyond these woods was not attempted owing to Flanks being in the air. 2nd Can Inf Bde was held up by Factory north of VILLERS LEZ CAGNICOURT but this and VILLERS LEZ CAGNICOURT were captured about noon.

Further advance was held up by BUISSY SWITCH which was not cleared up until evening. The whole advance on 1st Can Div front was held up beyond the RED LINE by Divisions on Flanks.

Our line for the night ran from FACTORY to BUISSY SWITCH East of VILLERS LEZ CAGNICOURT along BUISSY SWITCH to roads W. of BUISSY, then joining up with Railway line about 1500 yds S E [of] BOIS DE BOUCHE. Situation improves during early evening to right but Division on left meet with very heavy opposition and remain on RED LINE.

One battery (18pdr) from each of 2nd & 6th Bdes CFA did not fire in barrage but advanced in close support of 2nd and 3rd Can Inf Bdes respectively immediately after Zero. Remainder of these artillery brigades went forward after completion of Creeping Barrage. 1st Bde CFA keeps in close touch after completion of Creeping Barrage with 1st Can Inf Bde which was earmarked to go thru on 2nd Objective. 48th Bde RGA detached one six-inch howitzer battery to go forward with each infantry brigade: remainder of brigade (two sixty pdr batteries) remain under control CBSO until 3pm after which time they move forward to area in which [are] howitzer batteries.

39th Div Arty and 282nd Army Bde RFA pass to Corps Reserve on completion of Protective Barrage but stand ready to advance on short notice. 282nd A. Bde RFA is transferred to 4th CDA about 3pm. 39th Div Arty is asked for by 1st Can Div and go forward into action at dusk to support 2nd Can Inf Bde on left.

Artillery under control of CRA 1st Cdn Div are in position during night as follows:

> 1st Bde CFA – 3 batteries in vicinity of BUTT Copse (V7c) with 4th Bty at CAGNICOURT
> 2nd Bde CFA – 1000 yds NW VILLERS LEZ CAGNICOURT (P32c&d)
> 5th Bde CFA – 1000 yds W of CAGNICOURT (V8c & V14a)
> 6th Bde CFA – 500 yds W of CAGNICOURT (V8d & V14b)
> 174th Bde RFA – West of 2nd Bde CFA positions (P31)
> 186th Bde RFA – North of TRIGGER Copse (V7)
> 48th Bde RGA – North & North East of CROWS NEST (U5 & U6)

Prisoners captured by 1st Cdn Div to-day are over 2000.

Report from prisoner captured in early evening stated that 2 Regiments GUARDS were concentrating North of BUISSY with artillery in silent positions. This temporarily hastened the drawing up of more effective SOS lines to repel an assault from this direction.

Casualties in Div Arty were very light – One officer wounded and less than twenty ORs wounded.

The assault on the Drocourt–Queant Line was concluded successfully although the infantry had suffered very heavy casualties. The northern part of the line was particularly difficult to deal with because it involved crossing the long exposed crest of Mont Dury where the Canadians had to face strong enemy defensive machine gun fire. At the end of the day, the Drocourt–Queant Line had been overrun on a frontage of 7,000 yards. However, the fighting had been very hard against a stubbornly defensive enemy. Tanks, following up the infantry as they advanced, played a significant part. Members of the Canadian Corps won seven VCs that day.

NEUVILLE VITASSE/SUN QUARRIES September/3. Rain in early morning but clearing towards noon.

No further organized assault was made but our outposts on feeling their way forward found no enemy who would fight within several thousand yards of outpost line on north. Barrage on lower end of BUISSY Switch cleared up situation on south. Our posts were pushed forward quickly as far as line of CANAL DU NORD on East bank of which trenches were filled with Huns. Enemy batteries are well placed in position to cover approaches to CANAL and shell our troops pressing forward very heavily. During afternoon enemy blew up most of bridges over Canal.

4th Cdn Div on left press forward to line of CANAL. 63rd Division (Naval) are on Canal at our south boundary. They hold bridgehead East of

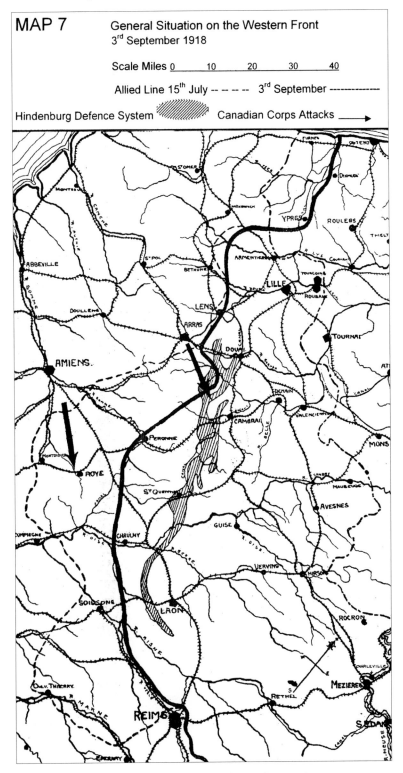

General Situation on the Western Front, 3 September 1918.

Inch en ARTOIS (which they hold) and TADPOLE Copse 1000 yds W of MOEUVRES.

Ammunition supply is good to forward positions. ARPs are established on main road 1000 yds NE CROWS NEST, at HENDECOURT Chateau, and at CAGNICOURT.

Orders received that 1st Can Div will be relieved in the line on nights of 3/4th & 4/5th September. Artillery relief is stated to be notified later and will probably not take place. 2nd Can Inf Bde is being relieved in Left Section by 6th Can Inf Bde to-night.

The 22nd Infantry Battalion had suffered the heaviest casualties, losing all of their officers and many other ranks. Subsequently, the enemy appeared to have withdrawn in order to prepare the next line of defence. General von Hindenburg described this withdrawal as one of the most disagreeable decisions forced on the German High Command.

General Currie had special praise for the 1st Canadian Division. In his diary, he assessed their success as 'one of the finest performances in all the war'. Nevertheless, he ordered the divisions under his command to continue their advance of 3 September in order to gain direct observation of the bridges over the Sensée River and the Canal du Nord. The abandonment of this part of the Hindenburg Line by the enemy was the result of a brilliantly organised assault by the Canadian Corps. The general situation and the advances made by the Allies from 15 July to 3 September 1918 are shown in Map 7.

CHAPTER SIX

Crossing the Canal du Nord

The Battle of Cambrai,
4 September – 7 October 1918

When the Hindenburg Line was breached from Drocourt to Queant, the Germans fell back on the Canal du Nord, their next defensive line. They destroyed the bridges and flooded the ground around parts of the canal. A little to the south, the canal was still under construction and dry, but the steep banks provided strong defensive positions.

The recent battles had taken their toll of men, especially in the infantry, and equipment; it was essential that the artillery, having been in almost continuous action for the past month, had their guns repaired and recalibrated before the start of the assault on the canal. Casualties had to be replaced in order to bring the units up to strength again, and training of replacements in their very specific roles was undertaken.

There was some confusion about the strength of the enemy positions in front of the canal. Mobile formations sent out to reconnoitre reported incorrectly that the enemy had withdrawn, thereby precluding preparatory bombardments by the artillery. This proved to be costly to the Canadians when they began their advance on the canal in preparation of crossing it.

While keeping their intentions hidden from the enemy, the Canadians sidestepped to the south, taking advantage of the dry section of the canal and overcoming the defenders. However, as the Canadians fanned out to attack the enemy positions at Bourlon Wood, they were resisted, forcing them to continue their advance in the left sector. The 1st Canadian Division bypassed Cambrai, leaving its capture to the 3rd and 4th Divisions.

------OOO------

Diaries for 4 September Onwards

SUN QUARRIES September/4. Dull with rain at intervals throughout the day.

At 11am warning given from 'G' Branch 1st Can Div that an operation may be expected shortly after dawn on Right Inf Bde Section and probably on left Inf Bde Section. This, if carried out, will be in conjunction with 63rd Division on right and 4th Can Div on left. Batteries are moved to forward positions at dawn and ammunition gun dumps increased. The operation will depend entirely on our troops reaching the East side of the Canal. Creeping barrage will carry infantry forward to BLUE LINE (approx. 3000 yds beyond Canal). All artillery are warned to prepare for this operation and to be able to carry it out at short notice.

Nothing is heard of this advance until GOC telephones from 1st Can Inf Bde HQs about 2pm that it is recommended to Corps Commanders to make the assault deliberately and on a wide front. Later in the day word is received that operation will not take place.

Canal du Nord is an obstacle. It is about 100 feet wide in places and all bridges are destroyed. East bank is strongly held by enemy m.g.'s.

HQs 2nd CDA assume command of artillery from HQs 1st CDA at 6pm at which time 2nd Can Div takes over from 1st Can Div. Grouping of artillery is slightly changed from hour of taking over by 2nd CDA due to Front being held by 3 battalions. 1st & 2nd Bdes CFA will form Centre Group 2nd CDA under CRA 1st Cdn Div with 39th Div Arty (Left Group) on left and 2nd CDA (Right group) on the right. Each Group will cover one battalion in the line.

Situation on Front remains stationary – our outposts being established on line of the Canal. 63rd Division are reported to be in MOEUVRES south of INCHY-EN-ARTOIS. Unofficial reports state enemy to the south is retiring to line of CANAL DU NORD.

1st Can Div (less Div'l Arty) on relief is withdrawn to WARLUS Area,

The 1st Canadian Division Infantry brigades, having played such a major part in storming the Drocourt–Queant Line, needed to have time and opportunity to rest and replace casualties. However, the artillery would be redeployed northwards to ensure that the territory up to the Canal du Nord occupied by troops from other divisions was secured.

SUN QUARRIES/CAGNICOURT September/5. Fair weather with scattered showers,

HQs 1st CDA move from SUN QUARRIES to dug-outs in QUEANT – DROCOURT Line near CAGNICOURT.

1st Brigade CFA Batteries move to vicinity of BUISSY where only forward guns were in action previously. 2nd Bde CFA moves 7th Battery to Eastern outskirts BUISSY about 1600 yds from CANAL. This location, if enemy were intending to hold line of CANAL very strongly, would receive very heavy shell fire. During the day everything points to general withdrawal of enemy artillery due possibly to 63rd Division on right having crossed canal at several points.

Batteries are all very comfortable in positions especially those about BUISSY. Strongly reinforced & cemented cellars offer very good protection for personnel.

Burning of our balloons continues – due probably to low clouds which hides enemy planes until actually over balloon. The new Fokker Biplane may possibly have some bearing on this subject.

General situation appears very satisfactory. Enemy is withdrawing from LA BASSEE to YPRES and from ARRAS to FISMES. Much speculation is being made on a possible withdrawal in the near future to the line of the MEUSE River.

Situation on our immediate Corps Front is more or less stationary. We are not to fight our way across the canal but if enemy offers little or no resistance our troops will immediately seize the Eastern bank.

There are plans to continue the offensive as soon as possible. Preparations to resume the attack continue without giving the enemy time to regroup in defence of the Canal du Nord. The enemy is being heavily engaged on fronts to the north and south and is hard-pressed to find the additional resources they require to defend this sector of the front.

CAGNICOURT September/6. Fair with thunder showers.

Orders are received that 1st Can Div Arty will be withdrawn during the night 6/7th September and march to DAINVILLE – AGNY – ACHICOURT Area. This probably is the forerunner of a new Drive. Where it will be no one seems to know but BETHUNE and Further South are both suggested.

Responsibility for the Group Front passes at 10pm.

1st & 2nd Bdes CFA and 1st CDAC march during the night. Roads are in very bad condition in forward area due to heavy rain about 7.30pm.

1st CDA has been in continuous action for the past month. The men need rest, their horses are worn out, and their guns urgently need maintenance.

CAGNICOURT/WARLUS September/7. Fair weather with occasional rain storms.

Units [of] 1st CDA are located in rear area as follows: 1st Bde CFA and 1st CDAC – DAINVILLE: 2nd Bde CFA – DAINVILLE WOOD: 1st CDTM Bde – ACHICOURT.

Horses due to heavy work during last operation are looking quite fatigued. Several days rest will put both horses and men in good shape.

HQs 1st CDA move during morning to WARLUS (where HQs 1st Can Div is now located.)

WARLUS September/8. Rain during most of the day.

Units are settling down in new locations to a well earned rest. As it is not known how long 1st CDA will remain out of the line, smartening and cleaning up is begun at once throughout the Divisional Artillery.

The time in reserve positions is taken up with testing anti-gas equipment and discussing the use of trench mortars following the recent successful campaigns.

WARLUS September/9. Fair with rain squalls at intervals.

Reports from Can Corps front indicate very free use of gas on forward area by the enemy. Preparations are being made for testing of all Small Box Respirators in Divisional Artillery at DAINVILLE Gas Chamber. During Lieut BYRONS absence on leave, Lieut GONNASON is acting Div Arty Gas Officer.

Situation on AMIENS Front appears to be slowing up. This is probably due to bad weather and also to the fact that the battle line is approaching the HINDENBURG Line.

Major CORBETT OC 1st Army Trench Mortar School meets Capt DEAN 1st CDTMO at this HQs during morning to discuss the Trench Mortar as used in AMIENS and ARRAS Operations.

The guns of 1st CDA are taken to the Petawawa Range for recalibration. Their accuracy must be maintained so that they can be used safely in close infantry support. The Small Box Respirators (SBRs) used by the troops have to be tested and individually fitted in the Gas Chamber at Dainville.

WARLUS September/10. Very high wind with rain squalls during the day.

Guns and howitzers of 2nd Bde CFA are calibrated at PETAWAWA Range. Transport to and from is carried out by lorries.

1st Bde CFA is having all SBRs tested and fitted at Gas Chamber in DAINVILLE under supervision of DGO and ACTING DAGO. Reliable gas NCOs from Bdes and DAC are assisting in this task.

Can Corps front remains normal. Gas shelling is decreasing, slight m.g. [fire] in BUISSY – CAGNICOURT Area. Heavy shelling of ARRAS is reported.

Hauling ammunition forward to a section of 9.2-inch Howitzers. Two Canadian siege batteries in the Canadian Corps Heavy Artillery were equipped with these guns. (*Courtesy of the RCA Museum*)

WARLUS September/11. Very cool but fair weather except for an hours rain during the morning.

Guns & howitzers of 1st Bde CFA are calibrated at PETAWAWA Range.

Two batteries (5th & 6th) of 2nd Bde CFA are testing respirators in DAINVILLE Gas Chamber.

WARLUS September/12. Rain throughout the day.

New areas are being reconnoitered for brigades. Present lines, if rainy weather persists, will soon be a quagmire. 1st Bde CFA find vacant standings in BERNVILLE and ask permission to move.

Testing of SBRs is still being carried on in DAINVILLE Gas Chamber.

WARLUS September/13. Fine weather.

Warning received that 1st Can Div will relieve 2nd Can Div in Right Sector, Can Corps front on nights 15/16th, 16/17th & 17/18th September. Command will pass at 10am on 17th September. Artillery relief will be on nights 16/17th & 17/18th with CRA 1st Can Div assuming command at 10am 17th.

Information from 2nd CDA HQs show gradual moving back of artillery owing to intense and continued gas shelling of forward areas in vicinity of BUISSY & BARALLE. Infantry are holding Forward Zone very lightly.

An advance by First American Army on ST MIHIEL Salient is reported. This will probably have great effect on rest of front owing to the advance being so close to German territory. From political & sentimental reasons the Hun will make a very great effort to stop further advance in this Sector.

WARLUS September/14. Fine weather with high winds.

Arrangements are made between 1st and 2nd CDAs regarding taking over ammunition and number of sections relieving on 1st and 2nd nights. Relief will be very simple as only one Brigade relieved is in the line – the other being in Divisional Reserve in CHERISY Area.

Further details regarding American advance are received. 13000 prisoners and 100 guns are now reported. The whole ST MIHIEL Salient is apparently wiped out.

WARLUS September/15. Fair weather but rather unsettled appearance.

Orders issued for relief of 2nd CDA by 1st CDA. 1st Bde CFA will relieve 5th Bde CFA in Divisional Reserve. 2Bde CFA will relieve 6th Bde CFA in the line.

About 9pm 1st Can Div HQs send out cancellation of relief of 2nd Can Div. 1st Can Div will remain in present area for the time being. What this means is apparent to all. The general impression given is that in spite of the fact that the 1st Cdn Div has been in two attacks during the past five weeks and has suffered a normal number of casualties, everyone without exception would much rather make preparations and carry out another assault than go into the line "to sit and hold" while battles are raging on either side.

The assault on the Canal du Nord was part of a carefully planned attack throughout the Western Front. However, the enemy was actively harassing Canadian troops stationed near to the Canal du Nord, forcing them to withdraw to a safer distance to avoid unnecessary casualties from machine-gun fire. It was unlikely that the enemy would attempt to counter attack here because they had flooded the low-lying ground in the immediate area of the canal banks and the Sensée marshes. Furthermore, they had destroyed all the bridges over the canal.

The Allies planned to make their assault further to the south where the canal construction had not been completed. It was still dry in this area and the land on either side remained free of floods. This sidestepping manoeuvre involved concentrating the troops in a small area from where the assault could begin, the preparations for which had to be made in great secrecy with troops moving at night wherever possible.

The Canadian Corps' front was to be only 2,600 yards long for the assault. It would be essential to conceal this concentration from the enemy because knowledge of it would enable them to bring down a very destructive artillery barrage that would severely disrupt the planned attack. The essential preparatory work for the assault on the canal took over ten days; the plan was thoroughly debated and the decision to go ahead was only agreed upon thanks to General Currie's very strong support.

WARLUS September/16. Dull weather.

Conference at Corps HQs during morning still further points to another operation in very near future. CRA is summoned to RA Can Corps HQs during afternoon to discuss artillery plans for an attack by Can Corps on BOURLON WOOD and area to the immediate north. This attack will be carried out in conjunction with the main attack by 3rd & 4th Armies. 1st & 4th Cdn Div's will attack with 3rd Cdn Div in Corps Reserve. Attack will be made to form a defensive flank for the operations of the 3rd & 4th Armies. Method of dealing with this operation differs somewhat from those for previous. Owing probably to the difficult nature of the ground in the vicinity of Jumping Off Line, the ideas of all commanders are solicited before finally deciding on plan to be adopted by the Corps. 24 hours are given for reconnaissance and report.

At 6pm a conference at Divisional HQs outlines roughly the disposition of troops for the attack. Reports are called for by to-morrow evening on any suggested improvements. The chief worry will probably be the crossing of the canal. Full information will be available regarding the work done on canal previous to war by to-morrow at the latest. In the meantime plans are to be made on the assumption that the canal is dry between two limits 1000 yds apart on Front given to Division.

WARLUS September/17. Fine weather after heavy thunderstorm during early morning.

Reconnaissance is made of area between INCHY-EN-ARTOIS and BUISSY. At the same time a distant observation is made on Canal bridges and dyke banks. Apparently in our area there is one road crossing canal on ground level – dyke banks being built up from ground and canal bed on ground level. This places a much simpler complexion on the operation from an artillery standpoint.

Battery areas are found which will enable Final Objective being covered from West side of Canal.

WARLUS September/18. Dull weather.

Nothing definite is received regarding contemplated operation which will be known as "BOURLON WOOD" Attack. Owing to the fact that the Canadians are merely making a Defensive Flank our action must be governed by wishes of main attacking forces – 3rd & 4th British Armies.

Conference of CRAs 1st & 4th Cdn Divisions is held at RA Can Corps office during the afternoon. It has now been found that 10 brigades of Field Artillery will be available for each Division – eight of these will probably be used for Creeping Barrage and two for exploitation on 1st Cdn Div Front.

There are as yet no plans for exploitation beyond BLUE Line: this will be forthcoming in the course of a day or so in all probability.

WARLUS September/19. Fair weather.

Brigade and Battery Commanders 1st CDA proceed to reconnoiter positions to perform Special Task from Zero to Zero plus 2.1/2 hours approximately. This task is necessitated by the GOC's 3rd Can Inf Bde wish to attack SAINS-LES-MARQUION from the East instead of from South or West. It will take the form of an Unrolling Barrage – Special Barrage will creep forward and form a Protective Barrage around the village. Under the barrage of the main field artillery groups, infantry will advance to First objective forming Flank facing SAINS-LES-MARQUION. As soon as First Objective is reached, Protective Barrage around the village will begin creeping west towards our own guns with infantry following up. It will be quite a unique operation as it will be a barrage within a barrage or an operation within an operation and will necessitate our infantry following a creeping barrage towards our own guns.

Warning issued by Division to the effect that WARLUS must be cleared by 10am to-morrow. Move will probably be to ACHICOURT.

WARLUS/ACHICOURT September/20. Rain squalls occasionally throughout the day: Weather becoming much cooler.

Move to good quarters in ACHICOURT during the morning.

Owing to operation taking place on 25th September, 1st & 2nd Bdes CFA and 1st CDAC will probably move forward to HENDECOURT Area to-morrow. Operation Order is issued but is later on cancelled owing to report from RA Can Corps and 1st Can Div that Z day will probably now be 28th inst. No apparent reason for units to crowd into forward area until it is necessary for ammunition packing.

Reports of enemy attempted attacks on front to the south near HAVRINCOURT. Enemy attack in force forces Division to our right out of MOEUVRES during early evening.

ACHICOURT September/21. Rain with high winds. This weather is more or less expected owing to equinoxial gales being due about this period.

Visit paid to RA Can Corps to endeavor to procure some early information regarding the operation but with no apparent results. Amm'n gun dumps are decided on – 750 rds per 18 pdr and 625 rds per 4.5 How. This amount appears abnormally large to dump in battery positions, some of which are within 1000 yds of Canal du Nord.

Resection of positions is being carried on during the day. This ought to be completed to-morrow at the latest.

1st CDAC moves during day and 1st & 2nd Bdes CFA during night 21/22nd to HENDECOURT Area.

ACHICOURT September/22. Wet weather continues.

Zero Day will now probably be 27th September. In order to get a suitable Zero Hour, Inf GOsC are asked to see what visibility exists about 3am. In spite of wet cloudy weather, it is reported that one is able to see objects quite distinctly at 50 yards and that trees are visible at 500. This fact may be a deciding factor in the selection of Zero Hour.

Resection of all positions is complete.

Ammunition hauling to Battle positions was commenced last night by 2 DAs on receipt of orders forward from Can Corps. This is being discontinued to-night.

ACHICOURT September/23. Weather appears to be clearing to fair.

Abnormal movement is reported in Forward Area both on roads by transport during the night and by reconnaissance parties by day. This has apparently been detected by the enemy who appears to have increased his harassing fire considerably.

It is now intended to enlarge the proposed BOURLON WOOD operation. Instead of a definite fixed piece attack, exploitation will be carried out to attempt to seize heights north and north west of CAMBRAI. 11th British Division is now attached to the Can Corps and will operate on the left.

Nothing further is being done towards preparation during the day except a careful study of maps and aeroplane photos by all headquarters.

Ammunition packing will be carried on by all artillery supporting 1st Can Div in the attack to-night. At least 200 rounds per gun must go forward on each of 1st three nights. Rear ARP is established on HENDECOURT – DURY Road from which point ammunition is taken forward to forward ARP West of BOIS DE BOUCHE by horse transport. Forward ARP supplies ammunition to pack animals only.

ACHICOURT September/24. Fair weather, cool.

Further instructions are received from RA Can Corps and 1st Can Div regarding BW [Bourlon Wood] operations.

CRA proceeds forward to visit Brigade commanders reference mobile artillery role.

Barrage maps are received late in the evening and are made ready for issue before midnight.

1st CDTM Bde moves from ACHICOURT to area near RIENCOURT.

ACHICOURT September/25. Fine weather.

Ammunition reports show gun dumps at Battle Positions increasing satisfactorily. Fair amount of shelling was encountered by several pack teams due it is reported to transport moving about on forward roads.

Barrage maps are delivered to all concerned during the morning. Further conferences are being held during the day regarding the action of close support brigades beyond the BLUE Line of the 1st Phase. 11th Division on the left is contemplating an advance under a Creeping Barrage for a certain distance. An attempt is being made to co-ordinate this into our plans in conference at 2nd Can Inf Bde's HQs ARRAS. Decision arrived at is to provide Creeping Barrage beyond the Yellow Line to line of CAMBRAI – DOUAI Road. Action of 39th Div Arty will be to leap-frog 1st & 2nd Bdes about Zero plus 9 hours – advancing after they have completed Final Protective Barrage.

ACHICOURT/V28doo September/26. Fine weather.

HQs 1st CDA moves during morning from ACHICOURT to dugouts south of BOIS DE BOUCHE V28doo.

Final preparations are being completed for BOURLON WOOD operation.

1st Can Div assumes command of Battle Front from 10am, also temporary command of 11th Div front on north from 10am until evening. Artillery covering Front of 1st Can Div from 10am – 10pm is 26th Army Bde RFA and 5th Bde CFA. At 10pm 9th & 10th Bdes CFA (3rd CDA) cover Front with 6 18pdr batteries. The front of 11th Division from 10am till evening is being covered by 174 Bde RFA (39th DA) and 52nd Army Bde RFA.

During last night up to 50% Field Artillery not engaged in protection of front moved to Battle Positions. Remainder move to-night. All guns of 26th & 52 Army Bdes RFA, 5th Bde CFA and 174 Bde RFA move to Battle Positions.

Prisoner captured reports relief opposite our front during last night and to-night. This is good news.

At 12 midnight 26/27th, although all artillery is not ready to open fire, practically all batteries are on their positions. Night remains normally quiet. Slight harassing of cross roads and roads which the enemy considers will most probably be used.

V28doo September/27. Fine weather throughout the day although at certain times it threatened rain.

All artillery reported in position and ready to open fire before 3am.

Zero Hour is 5.20am.

Barrage opened fairly well although one battery started about 30 seconds before the majority of guns. Shrapnel bursts are reported at effective height.

Intelligence

First reports from the front begin filtering in about 6am. Retaliation slight and almost entirely on general line of canal. Scattered shelling of battery areas which died away in half hour. A few guns of 4th Can Div are over canal about 7am (These belong to artillery detailed to rush forward to positions near canal shortly after Zero) Canal is apparently no great obstacle.

Move of 1st & 2nd Bdes CFA East of CANAL DU NORD

MONKEY PUZZLE Barrage on SAINS-LEZ-MARQUION having been shot out at 7.52am, 1st & 2nd Bdes CFA commence moving forward between 8am and 8.50am. By mutual agreement batteries of the two brigades are sent forward alternately. Between 10 & 11am Batteries are reported in W27. No great difficulty is experienced in Canal crossing although one howitzer of 2nd How Battery holds up traffic for considerable time at one stage.

Move of 39th Div artillery forward

First battery is released from Creeping Barrage at 11.43 and immediately limbers up and proceeds to assembly area. Before remaining batteries move off an uncertain situation arises south of MARQUION which necessitates 39th DA remaining in present position and dumping ammunition with a view to possible barrage to help out the situation. At 2pm information is received that BLUE Line is reached along practically whole front. 39th Div Arty is therefore ordered forward to Assembly Position East of Canal with a view to leap-frogging the 1st & 2nd Bdes CFA.

2nd Can Inf Bde operation beyond BLUE Line

At 3pm Creeping Barrage is placed within divisional Boundaries in 2nd Phase – commencing approximately on Yellow Line and ending in vicinity of DOUAI – CAMBRAI Rd. Air Report at 3.20pm shows our troops on both north and south of HAYNE COURT and going strong. Line of this road is reached with 11th Division in possession of EPINOY on left. On right 2nd C I Bde is forced to throw out Defensive Flank of practically 4000 yds owing to Division on right not advancing beyond BLUE Line. This had the appearance of a very "dirty" position as our right is exposed to MARCOING Line between RAILLENCOURT and SANCOURT. About 6.40pm enemy launches counter attack from this direction on HAYNECOURT which produced an obscure situation during the early portion of the night but later on found to be quite satisfactory.

Consolidation for the night
    Line held during the night is along DOUAI – CAMBRAI Road thence west along South Divisional Boundary to BLUE Line – in touch with 4th Can Div at junction of BLUE Line & Divisional Boundary and with 11th Division on eastern edge of EPINOY. Owing to length of Divisional Front to cover for SOS purposes, arrangements are made with 4th CDA to cover our South Boundary from BLUE line to X17c08 (SE HAYNECOURT). Remaining front is covered on right by 39th DA which moved forward at dusk to positions in W30b and on left by 1st & 2nd Bdes (Grouped under Lieut Col Anderson DSO) in positions used for Creeping Barrage placed on in early afternoon in HAYNECOURT Area.

Passing of 2nd CDA, 5th CDA & 52 Army Bde RFA & 26 Army Bde RFA
    On completion of barrage tasks detailed for main operation commencing 5.20am six of ten brigades of field artillery pass to other Divisions at times given below:

>   11.59am 26th & 52nd Army Bdes RFA to 11th Division
>   12.15pm 2nd CDA to 4th Can Division.
>   12.15pm 5th CDA to 3rd Can Division.

Positions during night 27/28th
Positions of batteries covering 1st Can Division during night are as follows:

1st Bde CFA	– W23
2nd Bde CFA	– W30 North of Bourlon Village
174th Bde RFA 39th Div Arty	– W30
186th Bde RFA	

The assault on the Canal du Nord went ahead according to plan. Only with the concentrated power of three Canadian Divisions (2nd Can Div remained in reserve) was it possible to ensure success. Another feature of this operation was the employment of heavy artillery for the initial barrage ahead of the advancing infantry. This was important because much of the field artillery had to move forward continually to maintain effective support for the infantry as it advanced.

A particularly innovative and courageous plan was to bring up one section of field guns into close support of the infantry as they crossed the open ground of the partly constructed canal. Firing over open sights, these 'sniping' guns were able to engage directly the machine gun nests the enemy was depending on to halt the infantry. The sound and effect of these guns firing from close behind contributed greatly to the morale of the advancing troops.

SPECIAL TASK of 1st Bty CFA

One section of 1st Bty CFA under command of Lieut McPHINNEY went forward about midnight 26/27th September and took up position in a hedge between INCHY-EN-ARTOIS and CANAL DU NORD in order to lend immediate support to our infantry in case they were held up at gap in canal. From what reports are now available infantry were greatly impressed and the risk incurred by taking guns to this position on Y/Z night was quite compensated by the confidence which infantry seemed to have in these lone guns. A few targets were seen and taken on but most of the fire was more or less into the bank of canal before infantry reached it and then "into the BLUE" beyond. About 70 rounds were fired in all with the loss to our teams of five or six horses.

GENERAL SITUATION on night 27/28

General line held by Canadian Corps to-night is as follows: North of FONTAINE – RAILLENCOURT (excl) – HAYNECOURT – EPINOY – OISY LE VERGER (all incl).

To the south XVII Corps are held up at GRAINCOURT but VI Corps (GUARDS Division) are at edge of MARCOING and NOYELLES.

V28doo September/28. Rain in early morning but clear to fine weather about noon.

Shortly after midnight 27/28th Orders received that Can Corps will continue the general advance at 6am with the primary object of completing the capture of the BROWN Line and securing the crossing over CANAL DE L'ESCAUT. 2dn Can Inf Bde is detailed for advance under a creeping barrage.

Owing to the difficulty arising from communication with forward area from our present location, CRA 39th Div is ordered to make all arrangements for placing a standing barrage from 6am if required and to be responsible for covering the entire Divisional Front while 1st & 2nd Bdes move forward to positions near HAYNECOURT from which Creeping Barrage may be carried to beyond ABANCOURT. 1st & 2nd Bdes move forward at dawn and arrive at new area without mishap. Creeping Barrage is fired by 1st & 2nd Bdes at 8.50 am but owing to heavy wire west of railway no appreciable advance is made and our line runs just East of DOUAI – CAMBRAI Road. 39th Divisional Artillery move up to positions forward of 1st & 2nd Bdes CFA (one brigade coming into action north of HAYNECOURT and about 1000 yds from our outposts)

Another barrage by 1st CDA & 39th DA scheduled for 12.30pm is not taking place owing to wire cutting operation commenced about 10am not being finished. Batteries stand ready for Creeping Barrage all afternoon and evening which does not take place. During entire day opportunity targets are being fired on by all batteries. Many "NF Calls" are received by 4.5 Howitzers.

Towards evening batteries increase gun dumps to 300 rds and settle down for night.

At 6.30pm and again at 7.15pm 4th Can Div to our right make minor attacks to push on to DOUAI – CAMBRAI Road within their boundaries but without much success. 11th Division to our left are holding BROWN Line – no advance being made owing to heavy m.g. fire

A 6-inch Howitzer being transported on a rail carriage. (*Courtesy of the RCA Museum*)

It is reported that an army of 9 Belgian, 6 British and 6 French Divisions attacked under leadership of the King of the Belgians and made good progress [further to the north].

V28d00 September/29. Dull and cool with high winds.

Practically the same order is issued by 1st Cdn Div early this morning as was issued yesterday. "Can Corps will continue the advance during the early morning and push on to seize the crossings over CANAL DE L'ESCAUT."

INTELLIGENCE

11th Division attacks at dawn but owing to heavy m.g. fire from left flank and shell fire from North of SENSEE River the attacking troops are forced to come back almost to Jumping Off Line. 1st, 4th & 3rd Canadian Divisions attacks at 8am under a Creeping Barrage. Altho this attack progresses at first the ground gained cannot be held owing to flanking m.g. fire. Very little progress is made along whole Corps Front during the day.

Enemy resistance is extraordinarily stubborn. M.G.'s appear to be in very large numbers and in spite of losses caused by our barrages enemy reinforcements are continually supplied.

ARTILLERY

Creeping Barrage is fired by the four artillery brigades – 39th Div Artillery and 1st Can Div Arty – commencing at 8am. This barrage lifts in 100 yds per 4 minutes to Eastern outskirts of ABANCOURT. In vicinity of railway barrage on left portion outstrips our infantry but Bn Commander considers that situation is well in hand. At this point enemy m.g.s begin to play in enfilade from valley NW of ABANCOURT. This appears to be the beginning of the "hold up" as further advance on left is out of the question as area is literally swept by m.g. fire.

About noon Infantry suggest that Sniping Gun be taken forward to deal with m.g.s. This is acted on by 174th Bde RFA but owing to exceptionally large number of enemy m.g.s it is rather difficult to do this task well.

Hard fighting takes place during the whole afternoon but dies down considerably towards evening. Enemy madly rushes masses of troops up valley from NE into the face of barrage concentration from our field [guns] and Heavies. Many opportunity targets are presented thru out the day and successfully engaged by the Field Artillery – in words of one BC [Battery Commander] "The killing to-day is wonderfully good and we don't mind waiting four years for a day like this."

OFFICER PATROLS

Practically the only reliable source of information while an attack is in progress is found to be by means of a patrol sent forward under an officer.

Firing a 9.2-inch Howitzer. (*Courtesy of the RCA Museum*)

This party gleans information from all possible sources and send back reports to nearest telephone by runner. Each brigade to-day send forward one such party and information which in former operations was very meagre, in this attack is quite plentiful. 39th Division Arty, when it was found that the situation on our flanks is obscure, send forward patrols to either flank and clear up the situation so far as our front is concerned.

In spite of "reliability" (apparent) of intelligence from various Divisional OPs throughout the day, it is found on summarizing Intelligence Reports during the evening that the most logical chronicle of events is furnished from our Officer Patrol Reports.

AMMUNITION

The supply of ammunition is very good. Guns are being well stocked from an ARP very close to majority of Battery Positions on CAMBRAI Road. In spite of difficulties experienced by DAs (as shown from continued demands on our ARP by their brigades) ammunition continues quite plentiful for 1st CDA Units. This is in a large measure due to foresightedness of officers in charge of ammunition branch; by clearing thousands of rounds from positions west of CANAL and by personally conducting lorry convoys to and from points where ammunition might be secured.

SITUATION ON CAN CORPS FRONT

Enemy is fighting very stubbornly and evidently attaches great importance to holding ground in salient north of CAMBRAI. He is making the fullest use of m.g.s and field guns but with apparent great number of casualties. Time after time Field batteries in the open were engaged and crews and teams destroyed. YNECOURT five 77s are lying with one gun limbered up and remaining limbers about 50 yards from guns. Teams and drivers are all there but dead.

GENERAL SITUATION

BELGIUM – King Albert's Army Corps is still advancing – PASSCHENDAELE – MESSINES – WYTSCHAETE – HOULHURST Forest all being in our hands.

CAMBRAI – ST QUENTIN – Americans and Australians attacked this morning and are going strong beyond HINDENBURG Line. CANAL DE L'ESCAUT is crossed at several points. This move is going to seriously endanger CAMBRAI and ST QUENTIN.

ARGONNE – French and Americans are continuing to advance on both flanks of FORÊT D'ARGONNE.

PALESTINE – General Allenby is approaching DAMASCUS and has cut the HEDZAS Railway.

MACEDONIA – Bulgaria's request for 24 hours armistice is turned down. Everyone awaits the next move as the state of military situation is nothing more or less than a rout.

The initial assault on the Canal du Nord has been successful despite the stubborn resistance of the enemy. Pressure is maintained in order to discourage a regrouping of their forces. At the same time, it is essential to relieve some of the units engaged in the initial operations, especially the infantry brigades that headed the assault.

V28doo September/30. Rain thru out the night and slight drizzle in early morning – clearing later in the day.

Infantry Relief is being carried out during early morning – 1st Can Inf Bde relieving 2nd Can Inf Bde in the line. Relief is completed during early morning before 3am.

OUTLINE OF OPERATIONS PLANNED FOR TO-DAY

Our Corps Line appears to run during night 29/30th September as follows: A13 central – A8 central – Jcn of BAPAUME & ARRAS Roads – Western outskirts NEUVILLE ST REMY – DOUAI Road – S20a00 – S13b80 – SANCOURT(incl) – NW along road thru X5b and – R34b and thence as before. XVII Corps (to right) is reported A20central – A26central – G2central.

Operations are being continued during early to-day with object of gaining bridgeheads over CANAL DE l'ESCAUT NE of CAMBRAI and of securing observation over SENSEE Valley.

Operations will be carried out in two Phases:

1st Phase. 3rd & 4th Can Divs are to attack in direction of RAMILLIES, ESWARS & CUVILLERS at 6am.

2nd Phase. 1st Can & 11th Divisions will attack towards ABANCOURT and FRESSIES about four hours later.

Second Phase will be more or less dependent on the success of the First Phase.

RA Can Corps are to arrange for as much Heavy Arty as possible to support First Phase and in Second Phase as much of same Heavy Artillery as possible to swing north in support.

No orders are issued to 1st CDA Units previous to carrying out of First Phase of operations as it is thought that probably the situation after First Phase will be changed to such an extent if successful that orders would have to be recast.

FIRST PHASE

3rd & 4th Can Divs attack at 6am under creeping barrage. Heavy artillery carry out a particularly heavy bombardment ahead of creeping barrage. All objectives except bridgeheads appear to have been held at about 9am but owing to heavy m.g. fire from flanks our infantry are forced to give way and line swings back almost to original line.

SECOND PHASE

At 10.50 it is decided that second phase should not be carried out until later on in the day when actual situation on 3rd & 4th Can Div Front is known. Conference is held at 1st CI Bde HQs W30d38 (GOC – CRAGSO1 and all artillery brigade commanders in attendance) to decide on barrage for the operation. GOC is hastily summoned to Corps Conference which CRA also attends. Decision reached is that 1st, 3rd & 4th Can Divs will attack on early morning 1st October under creeping barrage and 11th Division will conform.

NEW OPERATION

Creeping Barrage will be coordinated by RA Can Corps for attack by Can Corps to-morrow morning. Barrage Map is promised by 4pm but it does not actually arrive until 6.30pm when a tracing is brought along with practically nothing except boundaries of Divisions and 100 yard points on each boundary. This necessitates very hasty work by the 1st CDA office staff and even with quick work orders and barrage charts are not issued until 11.30pm.

INFANTRY DISPOSITION FOR ATTACK

1st Can Div attack will be carried out by 3rd CI Bde on right and 1st CI Bde on left. These units move up at dusk to assembly areas.

ADDITIONAL FIELD ARTILLERY

57th Div Arty (285 and 286 Brigades RFA) passes to control of CRA 1st Can Div during the evening and will be available for creeping barrage tomorrow. HQs 57 DA are at present resting in rear areas. The two brigades of 57DA under command of Lieut Col COOKES DSO (285 Bde RFA) form 57th Div Arty as it passes to 1st CDA. 57th Div Ammunition Column is believed to be available for ammunition feeding.

Diaries for October 1918

The advance continued but enemy resistance was stubborn. There was evidence of desperate measures on their part. Several divisions were in action in their attempts to stem the Canadian advance. At the same time, communications were difficult and this interfered with the urgent need to keep in touch with the infantry as they continued to encounter heavy fire from machine gun nests. Evidence of these difficulties was shown when 1st CDA detailed the 2nd Brigade CFA to concentrate a barrage on an area north-east of Abancourt. It was later found that the infantry commander had already made a direct request to 174th Brigade RFA, another British unit, to fire on the same target area. This situation was more effectively dealt with by putting 1st and 2nd Brigades CFA under the direct control of the General Officers in command of 1st and 3rd infantry brigades. This was to allow closer coordination between the artillery and the infantry as their rapid advance continued.

Telegraphic communication by wires laid on the ground, although vulnerable to damage by surface traffic, was still the preferred method of passing information. Wireless, although being gradually introduced, was still regarded as unreliable and potentially accessible to the enemy.

Enemy preparations for a counter attack were being anticipated by counter preparation measures by the artillery; a barrage was ordered just ahead of SOS lines. SOS lines were regularly updated to coincide with the foremost positions held by Canadian infantry. The barrages would smother areas for over half a mile to the rear of the enemy late at night and early in the morning when the counter-attacking forces were massing.

V28doo October/1. Rain through the very early morning but clearing towards dawn.

OPERATION

Detailed orders with barrage maps are issued under Operational Order #96 down to batteries. These have left 1CDA HQs office at 2330 last night by despatch rider who gets lost on the way and does not arrive at units until about 3am. This gives an extremely small margin to Battery Commanders to work out angles and ranges for guns.

Zero hour is 5am.

First reports show a hold up on left owing to heavy machine gun fire from northern flank. 2nd Brigade CFA is ordered to concentrate on railway line in m32a with all available guns from 8.50 – 9am. Later reports show that Battalion Commander on left got directly in touch with 174th Brigade RFA which was temporarily out of touch with HQs and arranged a barrage to commence on railway on m32a at 8.50am resting there for ten minutes and then lifting in 100x lifts per 4 minutes to Final Objective in m27d NE of ABANCOURT. Even this does not clear up the situation in vicinity of railway and ABANCOURT.

On the right infantry advances with practically no opposition through BLECOURT, BANTIGNY and CUVILLERS to sunken road 1000 yards NE of CUVILLERS in their stride. Machine gun fire from N and NE and from flanks forced our men to withdraw slowly to CUVILLERS & BANTIGNY. Situation for considerable time was very uncertain. Elements of our troops

Canadian gunners in action. (*Public Archives of Canada*)

were everywhere in ABANCOURT, BANTIGNY and CUVILLERS but enemy machine guns were still holding out in isolated spots and inflicted very heavy casualties on our troops moving across the open.

Mobile 18pdr Bty (3rd Bty CFA) advances at Zero in support of 16th Can Bn which is exploiting beyond the Final Objective to Spur East of CUVILLERS. Advance goes well but battery retires hurriedly from vicinity of BLECOURT when flanking machine guns open fire and take up position SW of SANCOURT. Major C V STOCKWELL Commander of 3rd Bty CFA is wounded on reconnaissance duty at CUVILLERS.

SITUATION TOWARDS NOON

Attack and counter attack are the order of the day from 11.00 until 15.00. Our troops reported in ABANCOURT and again driven out. Concentrations of heavies and field artillery are placed on different areas here and there throughout the zone of attack. Enemy makes use of the ravines and valleys from NE. Time after time masses of enemy are caught in our barrages. The killing must have been extremely heavy to enemy. Opportunity targets kept field guns in 1st Brigade CFA in action practically the whole day. Total expenditure for the day is later found to be 25,000 [rounds] for field artillery covering 1st Canadian Division.

MOVES OF BRIGADES DURING DAY AND EARLY MORNING

All batteries were ordered during early evening yesterday to move to positions where ranges did not exceed 6500 yards on Final Protection Barrage. This necessitates 1st Brigade CFA to move forward to new positions north and south of HAYNECOURT. Remaining four brigades with 1st Can Div are OK for barrage.

Following the 'shooting out' of the barrage all 2nd Brigade CFA moves to valley west of SANCOURT about 11.00. Several Btys 3rd CDA commence advancing but later stopped owing to uncertainty of situation and withdrew to original positions.

DISPOSITION OF FIELD ARTILLERY SUBSEQUENT TO BARRAGE WORK

1st and 2nd Brigades CFA at 11.30 are placed under control of GOs C 3rd and 1st Canadian Infantry Brigades respectively to advance to positions for more effective support as situation presents. Brigade Commanders maintain touch during afternoon with Infantry Brigadiers.

57th and 39th Division Artilleries are supporting artillery covering 3rd and 1st Canadian Infantry Brigades respectively. These artilleries are ordered to keep in close touch with Infantry Brigade HQs and to move forward if necessary conforming to moves of mobile artillery brigades but at longer ranges. Sanction for moving forward must be obtained from HQs 1st CDA.

ARTILLERY POLICY DURING NEXT FEW DAYS

Late in afternoon Artillery Instruction #38 is issued to units detailing artillery policy to be followed.

The following description of counter preparation, combing back and forth on enemy positions where a counter attack is being prepared, is a further example of the need for great accuracy and control of field guns.

COUNTER PREPARATION

Owing to reports from many sources Corps Commanders consider that enemy may attempt an attack to regain what he has lost in last few days. In today's fighting prisoners of 13 enemy divisions are identified. Counter preparation is accordingly ordered by RA Canadian Corps to be put on at 19.15 today and at 04.30, 05.00 and 05.30 tomorrow. Procedure will be Two minutes on SOS lines, lift 200 yards per 2 minutes for 5 lifts then back on SOS lines for 3 minutes. Rate of fire will be normal.

SIGNALS 1st CDA

In spite of almost insurmountable difficulties 1st CDA Signal Section kept up communication throughout the operations. HQs 1st CDA was in close proximity to all groups at Zero Hour on 27th but as brigades advanced more and more wire had to be laid and patrolled. From 1st Brigade CFA in HAYNECOURT to this office over 8 miles of wire was laid on 29th. Personal supervision by Off i/c Sigs 1st CDA was mainly responsible for the good work. From early to late each day he moves about over the whole area laying out new lines and later on when these were laid poling up all lines to keep them clear of transport and riders. Flanking units were continually using our lines throughout the operations showing clearly the quality of work done by 1st CDA Signal Section.

The foremost infantry units have advanced over 10,000 yards from the crossing of the Canal du Nord in the first two days. However, the enemy is managing to resist very strongly at this stage and is threatening counter attacks. In order to provide accurate supporting fire, some field artillery is moved up to within 6,500 yards of the front. At the same time, counter preparation against the massing areas used by counter attacking forces is carried out as planned. This brings swift retaliation by enemy counter batteries.

The intention is to begin a pincer movement on Cambrai, which is still in enemy hands. The British 24th Division will move forward on the south side of the city which will threaten the enemy with the risk of encirclement should they decide to stay there. However, fierce resistance is encountered throughout the area as the Germans prepare a fighting retreat.

V28doo October/2. Cool and windy with rain towards evening.

COUNTER PREPARATION

In accordance with Canadian Corps instructions Counter Preparation was put on at 04.30, 05.00 and 05.30 each time of which drew considerable retaliation.

INFANTRY RELIEF

Portion of the 3rd Canadian Division, entire 4th Canadian Division and about 800 yards of 1st Canadian Division Fronts is relieved by 2nd Canadian Division during night of 1st/2nd October. Artillery boundary is adjusted at 10.00 today. Artillery grouping remains the same on 1st Canadian Division Front each group covering one battalion.

INTELLIGENCE

Front remains fairly quiet throughout the day. Abnormal transport and gun movement is noticed by Forward Observation Officers in rear enemy areas – otherwise fair amount of individual movement.

At 13.50 RFA Brigade Colonel from vicinity of EPINOY observes white Very Lights from ABANCOURT. This is corroborated by inf obs reports which state succession of white Very Lights from m33a&e. This is thought to be 'A' Company 1st Infantry Brigade which is reported to have advanced into the 'Blue'. An operation to relieve these men is proposed but will not take place owing to nil observation by contact plane sent over ABANCOURT.

11TH DIV OPERATION

11th Division are arranging to carry out an attack towards the wire running E & W south of CANAL DE LA SENSEE. Cooperation of two brigades of our artillery is requested and is given providing no SOS is in progress on own front. Our part is merely to search and sweep an area between railway and wire on the front of the attack from Zero to Zero plus 25. Zero hour is at 23.59 although at first thought to be 21.30 tonight or 05.30 tomorrow morning. 39th Divisional Artillery carry out this operation.

THREATENED ATTACK BY ENEMY

Towards evening considerable excitement is raised at Corps HQs by statement of enemy officer prisoner who states that enemy will attack tonight. When this is borne out by heavy attack on 2nd Canadian Division about 18.30 Corps Commander orders Counter Preparation which is put on along Canadian Corps Front. Everything quietens down quickly. To create alarm and despondency to enemy plans for the morning RA Canadian Corps give orders for Counter Preparation tomorrow morning at 05.00.

SOS LINE

SOS Line along Div'l Front is 200 yards beyond railway line for the night. This move is to enable our patrols to get out to the line of the railway during darkness.

GENERAL SITUATION

Another portion of line is now beginning to fluctuate. Enemy is now withdrawing from LENS to LA BASSEE.

REPORTS FROM OTHER FRONTS

PALESTINE. Captures now up to 67,000. Damascus is now in our hands. ST QUENTIN is now reported in hands of the French.

V28doo October/3. Fair weather and not so cool as during past few days.

INFANTRY RELIEF

33rd Inf brigade of the 11th British Division relieves 2nd Canadian Infantry Brigade in the line through the night 2nd/3rd; relief being completed during the very early morning. At hour of completion this portion of front passes to command of GOC 11th Br Division thereby releasing 1st Canadian Divisional Infantry from any line responsibility.

ARTILLERY ARRANGEMENTS

Coincident with hour of completion of relief mentioned above, Field Artillery covering 1st Canadian Division becomes a group under 11th Division Artillery and remains covering the same front under command of CRA 1st Canadian Division. In view of probable withdrawal of 1st CDA, CRA 59th Division is warned that in this event he will assume command of 1st CDA Group less 1st and 2nd Brigade CFA and will cover Right Infantry Brigade 11th Division. Further, 1st and 2nd Brigades CFA until withdrawal will be superimposed over their respective sub group zones so that they can be withdrawn any time without affecting artillery dispositions on the front.

INTELLIGENCE

At 05.00 Counter Preparation is put on along entire Corps Front. Retaliation is slight. Considerable shelling of EPINOY takes place throughout the morning.

11h Division in their attack during the night reached a belt of wire not shown on the map and which was about 400 yards South of their objective.

33rd Infantry Brigade notify us that their patrols are pushing out to the railway line during the night 3rd/ 4th. SOS lines until further orders will be 200 yards beyond railway line across 1st CDA Group Front.

Front appears to be quietening down very quickly. It is thought that enemy is only too anxious to have it do so as he urgently needs reinforcements for his other fronts.

GENERAL SITUATION

Withdrawal continues between LENS and AUBERS. LENS is now entirely in our hands as is SALOME and ILLIES north and east of LA BASSEE.

Considerable advance between CAMBRAI and ST QUENTIN.

Resistance is increasing in BELGIUM but advance continues. We are close to ROULERS on the NW.

Preparations are made for 1st CDA to be relieved by the 11th Division artillery and for its brigades to hand over progressively before they move away. It is clear that having been at the forefront of the fighting since the beginning of September, they must be allowed to recuperate. However, they are only moving to a quieter sector of the front where the enemy is unlikely to attempt to mount a counter attack because there are many water obstacles, lakes and rivers, which would make ground operations difficult.

V28doo October/4. Dull and very cool weather. Slight ground mist.

GOC 1st Canadian Division proceeds on leave during early morning. Brigadier Gen THACKER CMG DSO CRA 1st Canadian Division assumes command of Division during his absence.

Owing to shortage of senior officers amongst brigades it is decided to leave Lt Col Anderson with his brigade and to have HQs 1st CDA cross functioning as a Group HQs under 11th Division Artillery. This takes place 1200 noon – 1st CDA HQs handing over to 39th Division Artillery HQs.

WITHDRAWAL OF 1st CDA

Warning is given from RA Canadian Corp during early afternoon that 1st and 2nd Brigades CFA will be withdrawn after 1900 o'clock and that 1st CDA will march to WANCOURT Area during the night. This order is confirmed later in the day.

During the withdrawal units experience very heavy bombing and shell fire. Medical Officer of 1st Brigade CFA is killed leaving the outskirts of HAYNECOURT and the French interpreter wounded.

No details are yet available as to number of casualties. Heavy bombing is heard in direction of MARQUION where CAMBRAI – ARRAS Road crosses the canal.

RELIEF OF 4th DIVISION ARTILLERY

Warning is received that 1st Canadian Division Artillery will relieve 4th Division Artillery on nights 5/6th and 6/7th Oct. 4th (British) Division is

A battery of 13-pdr anti-aircraft guns. (*Courtesy of the RCA Museum*)

now holding a front of approximately 12,000 yards between LA SCARPE and CANAL DU NORD. This is apparently a flooded area with only a few crossings mainly at SAILLY.

The brigades' march westwards comes under heavy attack from the air and from enemy artillery until they are across the Canal du Nord. Although there are some casualties, their survival during this march seems almost miraculous. Finally, they are able to bivouac near Wancourt, a village about ten miles west of the Canal du Nord.

V28doo October/5. Dull and very cool.

MARCH OF 1st CDA

Units have very exciting march during the night 4/5th [harassed] by incessant bombing between gun positions and CANAL DU NORD. Brigade Commanders remark that it is miraculous how the units escaped without casualties beyond those incurred by HQs 1st Brigade CFA about 1000 yards West of HAYNECOURT. In addition to Medical Officer being killed, the French interpreter and Lieut Davies were wounded. From accounts given by Lieut Col PIERCY DSO commanding 1st Brigade CFA, he with his headquarter officers were riding when attacked by a very low flying plane. Six bombs were dropped the last of which fell on the party wounding or killing every horse and all members of the party except Lt Col PIERCY and his groom.

Remainder of march made without incident beyond bombing at Canal crossing. March of #3 Section 1st Canadian Division Ammunition Column not made until 9am owing to "tie up" in orders. All units are bivouacked in WANCOURT area by noon.

RELIEF OF 4th DIVISION ARTILLERY

Units prepare to relieve 4th Division Artillery during the day and at night First Sections relieve without mishap. Brigades owing to their being one in Right and other in Left Group are far removed from each other in position. 1st Brigade on completion of relief will be in DURY Area and 2nd Brigade in MONCHY Area.

RELIEF OF ARMY BRIGADES

77th Army Brigade RFA which with 2nd Brigade CFA forms Left group and 189th Army Brigade RFA which with 1st Brigade CFA forms the Right Group are being relieved on nights 7/8th and 8/9th October by a 4th CDA Brigade and by 1st Brigade CFA relieved on same nights by remaining 4th CDA Brigade. This double relief is being carried out to place Divisional Artilleries in Group by themselves, 4th CDA on right and 1st CDA on left.

1st CDA TO XXII CORPS

1st CDA on coming into WANCOURT area passes to control of XXII Corps. This is merely temporary as Canadian Corps expect to relieve XXII Corps about 10th Oct. Reliefs are supposed to be carried out under orders of 4th Division Artillery (XXII Corps).

GENERAL

The general idea of all moves taking place at present appears to be to place Can Corps in a quiet sector to rest and "lick our wounds". Reinforcements must be absorbed and a front such as the one 1st Canadian Division is taking over is just as good for this purpose as a rest area. Water apparently separates our outposts from the enemy at almost every point except the bend in the river near SAILLY-EN-OSTREVANT. No great activity will probably take place on our part unless enemy decides to withdraw – indications of which are now reported.

V28do0 October/6. Dull and cool. Rain at intervals.

Summer time ends at midnight 5/6th October – two minutes after 24.59 of yesterday becomes 00.01 of today.

RELIEF OF ARTILLERY

Relief of 1st Sections is carried out without mishap during night of 5/6th and of remaining sections before 22.00 today. Our brigades during the night will be under HQs 4th Div Artillery but pass to HQs 1st CDA at an early hour tomorrow.

All reliefs scheduled to begin tonight are cancelled owing to contemplated operation on morning of 8th October. This means that 77th and 189th Army Brigades RFA will not be relieved on nights 7/8th and 8/9th October by 4th CDA.

BATTERY POSITIONS

Positions in new area appear to be quite good. All positions have plenty of Dug out accommodation. Enemy Counter Battery work is reported to be quite weak. Good roads exist to vicinity of all positions. All units should get quite rested in this area provided that no general retirement on part of enemy takes place – indications of which are at present very plentiful.

1st CDA HQs moves to another location to be on hand when operations begin in this sector. It is desirable for 1st CDA and other units available in support to harass the enemy, but infantry are not to advance until they decide to withdraw. Thereafter, Canadian troops will follow up as closely as possible to ensure that the enemy is given no opportunity to rest and regroup. To encourage the enemy to consider withdrawal as the best option, a dummy attack (it is called a Chinese attack here) is prepared with appropriate artillery preparation. It would be unwise to make a formal assault across so many water obstacles.

The enemy is occupying a salient that is being progressively squeezed from the north and the south. 1st Canadian Division has the task of harassing their southern flank. It involves the northern part of the Queant–Drocourt defensive line. This was broken earlier on further south at its hinge point with the Vis-en-Artois Switch on the approach to the Canal du Nord.

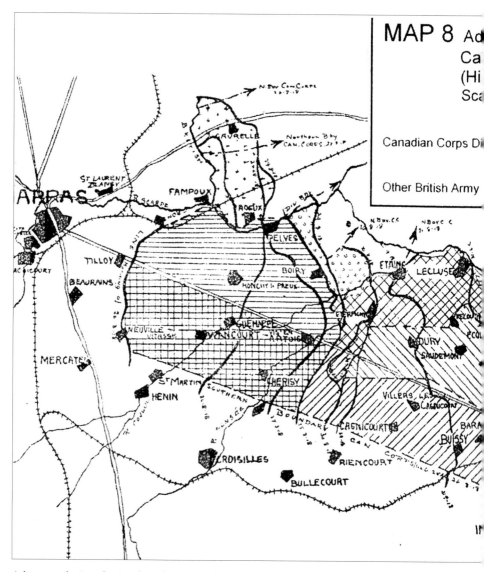

Advances during the Battles of Arras and Cambrai.

V28doo/ LES FOSSES FME SOUTH of MONCHY LE PREUX
October/7. Dull with rain. Slight mist.

Artillery HQs closes at V28doo and opens LES FOSSES FME South of MONCHY at 10am, Command of artillery covering 1st Can Division passing to CRA 1st Canadian Division at the same hour.

CHINESE ATTACK

In conjunction with operation by 8th Division on the left and southern portion of First Army, 3rd Army and Fourth Army, a dummy attack will be carried out tomorrow morning at SAILLY-EN-OSTREVANT. Creeping

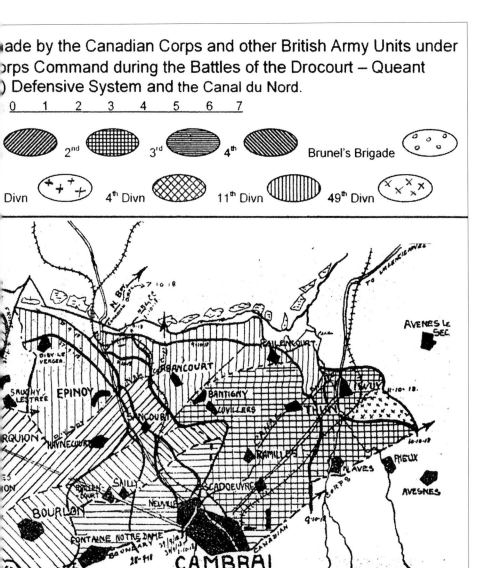

barrage with some smoke will be put on from the village to the Queant Drocourt line to the NE. Orders for this operation were issued by 4th Divisional Artillery previous to relief.

ENEMY RETIREMENT

In view of success of minor operation to our left when BIACHE ST VAAST and GLOSTER WOOD were captured this morning it is thought altogether likely the enemy will attempt a general retirement along the front to the north. Instructions are issued by last despatch rider that closest touch will be maintained with enemy. Crossings over SENSEE will be reconnoitered to pass over artillery to cover Southern outskirts of DOUAI.

The advances made by the Canadian Corps and the other British units under their command during the period from 26 August up to and after 7 October are shown in Map 8.

CHAPTER SEVEN

German Forces in Fighting Retreat

Overcoming the Last German Stronghold at Mont Houy, 8 October – 11 November 1918

The advance of the Canadian and other Allied forces continued, but the Germans did not give ground easily. In retreat, they laid waste the roads and railway lines, destroyed crops and set fire to villages. Later, 1st CDA went into reserve and the other Canadian divisions overwhelmed Mont Houy, a stronghold near Valenciennes. The Germans attempted negotiations during this period but their armies continued to fight as if they were making a tactical retreat. In the end their plenipotentiaries agreed to all Allied demands and hostilities ended at 11 a.m. on 11 November. The Canadians, meanwhile, occupied Mons and continued onwards until the time agreed in the armistice arrangements.

------ooo------

Diaries for 8 October Onwards

LES FOSSES FME October/8. Dull and very cool. Slightly misty.
CHINESE ATTACK

In conjunction with operations on the immediate left and distant right a dummy attack under a creeping barrage is put on from SAILLY to Queant Drocourt Line to north east. 3rd Canadian Infantry Brigade take advantage of this feint to push out posts to West of SAILLY. These are heavily shelled when found by the Hun. Enemy resents very much our having posts on his edge of the SENSEE and even more so when we push them further forward.

Intermittent flurries of shell fire by both enemy and ourselves are the order of the day from morning to evening in SAILLY area. Enemy is not successful in any of his sorties to drive our posts in.

GENERAL

Enemy activity is below normal on front except at SAILLY thru out the day. A few scattered flurries of whizz bangs on LE CLUSE. No shelling of rear areas is reported.

Operations on a large scale commences at dawn against enemy positions between CAMBRAI and ST QUENTIN.

The policy of not attacking the enemy here is maintained, but troops are detailed to move forward to occupy any posts from which the enemy has withdrawn. With ammunition dumps still being rather far to the rear, it is very tiring for the horses to carry forward the necessary supplies. Intense activity by the 3rd Canadian Division in the relief of Cambrai is reported further to the south.

LES FOSSES FME October/9. Dull with rain in early morning but clearing later in the day.

Day is one of practically no activity. Very little enemy movement is reported.

All batteries are settling down well and making themselves comfortable. If the situation demands much fire, our horses will not improve much as ammunition dumps are quite a long distance to the rear: more particularly in Right Group. As soon as 4th CDA take over Right Group an ammunition dump will probably be established at ST SERVINS FME which should improve matters.

"DROCOURT – QUEANT" OPERATION

Late in afternoon orders are received that 3rd CI [Canadian Infantry] Brigade will push out patrols during the night 9/10th and occupy DROCOURT – QUEANT Line. If this involves heavy fighting our troops will fall back to present outposts.

Instructions are received from RA XXII Corps that practically all heavy artillery will be available for use as 1st Canadian Division desires. This is later found to comprise our own two affiliated heavy brigades – 19th and 50th Brigades RGA.

At a conference at 3rd Canadian Infantry Brigade HQs about dusk it is decided that the arty preparation will be a series of heavy bursts of fire at odd intervals from 20.00 to midnight. These flurries are later extended to 02.30 when Zero Hour is notified as being 03.00 tomorrow morning.

Arrangements are also made by Left Group to have one 18pdr bty in direct telephone communication with 13th Can Inf Brigade HQs so that after Zero if any point holds up our bombers it can be dealt with quickly and efficiently.

GENERAL

CAMBRAI is captured by 3rd Canadian Division. Attack is reported to be going wonderfully well further south.

It is decided to sound out the enemy in the remainder of the Queant–Drocourt Line with a formal assault by the 3rd Infantry Brigade. Despite a series of very heavy artillery bombardments, the Germans regroup after the successful occupation of the line by Canadian troops. Their counter attack forces them back to previous outposts secured in earlier attacks.

LES FOSSES FME October/10. Dull and slightly misty.

ATTACK BY 3rd CANADIAN INFANTRY BRIGADE

Hurricane shoots continue until 02.30 for 5 minutes each. 15 minute concentration commences at Zero on QUEANT – DROCOURT Line then lifts to heights North East and continues at Slow until Zero plus 75.

Infantry patrols have little difficulty in entering the Q.D. Line where they remain until 07.30 when heavy counter attacks force them back to original posts. Remainder of the day passed without incident except heavy shelling of our SAILLY POSTS.

ARTILLERY RELIEF

Several times during the morning XXII Corps RA orders are issued changing plan of relief. In the end it is decided to have 3rd Brigade CFA relieve 77th Brigade RFA and 4th Brigade CFA relieve 189th Army Brigade RFA. Relief is carried out "in toto" on the one night and completed about 21.00. At midnight 10/11th Command of Right Group passes from 1st Brigade CFA HQs to HQs 4th CDA.

SITUATION

About 16.00 enemy commences heavy bombardment of SAILLY Area. The persistency of this shelling in the end gives one the impression that enemy is attempting to get rid of his ammunition prior to evacuating.

As anticipated earlier, the enemy is retiring to straighten their line by relinquishing the remainder of the Queant–Drocourt Line. This will enable them to take up a more easily defended position to the north of the Canal de la Sensee. However, they are still fighting strongly, and despite the rumoured peace negotiations, they are pillaging and burning towns, villages and crops as they retire. The 1st and 4th Canadian Divisions are now advancing and consolidating the broad front of the Allied advance north and south of Cambrai. The Canadians are following the retreating Germans as closely as they can. There is a reason for this other than to liberate friendly civilians and territory: if the Germans do not have time

A 15-inch BL Siege Howitzer. (*Courtesy of the RCA Museum*)

to prepare and consolidate in defensive positions farther to the rear, then they cannot impose any meaningful delay that will force the Allies to halt and prepare another major attack, which will takes days, if not weeks. There is a chance that if they are pressed firmly enough, the cohesion of their planned withdrawal will break down and the whole thing could degenerate into a rout.

LES FOSSES FME October/11. Dull with rain at intervals throughout the day.

ENEMY WITHDRAWAL

About 07.30 message is received from 8th Divisional Artillery to our left reporting that in their attack this morning their infantry found the QUEANT – DROCOURT Line practically unoccupied. Enemy had retired during the night to the line of the CANAL immediately West of DOUAI.

Orders are issued by Division "G" on receipt of practically the same message to both infantry brigades in the line to send out strong patrols at once and push forward if no strong opposition were found. Artillery teams are "standing by" close to their gun positions.

Only slight opposition is encountered and our infantry presses on towards the line of the CANAL DE LA SENSEE which is not quite reached before nightfall. The following line is held for the night HAMEL – ESTRÉE – LEMONT – NOYELLE sous BELLONNE – MONT GEORGE (S. of VITRY-EN-ARTOIS) 8th Division on left conforms to our line.

ARTILLERY POSITIONS

Artillery moves forward late in the afternoon. The crossing of the flooded area is dependent on the bridging done by Engineers. Bridge at SAILLY-EN-OSTREVANT is completed about 16.30 o'clock and three 18pdr batteries of the 2nd Brigade CFA cross over to positions N. of SAILLY. Positions occupied during the night are as follows:

RIGHT GROUP –	1st Brigade CFA – HQs LECLUSE Btys J85d, P6a&c
	4th Brigade CFA – HQs LECLUSE Btys – P12 & 18
	(N. of RECOURT)
LEFT GROUP –	2nd Brigade CFA – HQs SAILLY Btys J20d, J21c, J32a
	3rd Brigade CFA – HQs HAMBLIN Btys I30
	(E. of HAMBLIN)

All wagon lines move to gun positions vacated and DACs to Dump Area

GENERAL POLICY

The policy governing our action tonight and tomorrow will be one of following closely the enemy in his retirement. It is thought that he will hold the line from ARLEUX north of the CANAL and thence along the CANAL. Tomorrow at dawn 1st Canadian Division is to press on to line of canal seizing a bridgehead if possible and on the line reorganize and send out strong Reconnaissance Patrols preliminary to crossing.

GENERAL

Enemy appears to have no fear for what he does now being repaid him shortly. In spite of his request for an armistice he is consistently burning and pillaging the country he gives up. DOUAI and many other towns are now in flames.

The enemy is retiring beyond the Canal de la Sensée at this point. However, the bridges across rivers and lakes and the tracks leading up to them are only suitable for one-way traffic. This makes any supply operations servicing the far side of the canal vulnerable to enemy artillery. They are continuing to engage Allied operations with harassing artillery fire.

LES FOSSES FME October/12. Misty with rain throughout the day.

Roads are rapidly softening. Cross country tracks are very soft and will be unfit for use if this rain continues.

ENEMY RETIREMENT

Commencing at dawn our infantry push forward toward CANAL DE LA SANSEE. Opposition is not great although isolated machine guns are encountered here and there. Line of canal is reached about noon. During the early morning 2nd Can Inf Brigade encroach on area of 56th Division to the right capturing ARLEUX and Trench System running north to the canal.

Artillery push forward closely following the infantry. Some difficulty is experienced during the early morning by left artillery brigade commander in keeping touch with the Battalion HQs of infantry covered. Guns are however moving well forward and carry out effective harassing fire beyond Canal Line until touch with infantry is maintained.

Enemy carries out very violent harassing fire during the day on area immediately west of canal by 77s & 10.5cm calibres. During the early night gas is fired indiscriminately over whole forward area.

SOS Line for field artillery during the night is 300x east of the canal.

ARTILLERY POSITIONS

At dusk Field artillery are in position as follows:

RIGHT GROUP　–　1st Brigade CFA – as for yesterday
　　　　　　　　　4th Brigade CFA – HQs LECLUSE Btys Sth Bank of
　　　　　　　　　river between LECLUSE & HAMEL
LEFT GROUP　–　2nd Brigade CFA – HQs S edge NOYELLE Btys
　　　　　　　　　Valley immediately S. of NOYELLE
　　　　　　　　　3rd Brigade CFA – HQs MONT GEORGE Btys
　　　　　　　　　VITRY- EN-ARTOIS & BREBIERES

Wagon Lines are in every case at or close to gun positions.

AMMUNITION

Supply of ammunition although satisfactory at present may become serious if enemy places much shell fire on bridges at SAILLY & TORTEQUENNE. At each point bridges permit only one way traffic and at SAILLY approaches for quarter mile on either side are only one way. An attempt will be made to establish ammunition dump for Left Group north or NE of SAILLY – lorries being brought across river at TORTEQUENNE. Ammunition Dumps at present are for Right Group Sth of LECLUSE close to Battery areas and for Left Group sth of bridge at SAILLY. Supply at dumps is quite good.

Although the enemy is making a tactical retirement in the north of this sector, they clearly intend to maintain a strong defence of the east side of the Canal de la Sensée in order to maintain this southern flank of the salient.

LES FOSSES FME October/13. Rain and mist. Heavy rain throughout the night and early morning, clearing later in the day to rain at intervals.

ENEMY WITHDRAWAL

Enemy withdrawal continues north of Divisional Sector but line remains stationary on CANAL DE LA SENSEE. Strong patrols are pushed forward during early morning but find enemy machine guns in strength on east bank of canal and in Trench System immediately east.

Right Infantry Brigade have camouflage barrage put on at 06.15 which continues to 06.30. This draws considerable shell fire in retaliation. Heavy machine gun fire opens on our patrols as they push forward.

ARTILLERY

Batteries except those of 1st Brigade CFA remain in positions of yesterday. 1st Brigade CFA moves into the line NE of TORTEQUENNE during the afternoon to obtain shorter range for prospective creeping barrage to be laid down tomorrow morning on Right Infantry Brigade Front.

Ammunition supply is much better today. Dump is established on North bank of river and East of SAILLY. This is supplied by lorry (Lorry route via LECLUSE & TORTEQUENNE).

LES FOSSES FME October/14. Rain throughout very early morning but clearing to fine weather at dawn and continuing during the day. Roads dry up very quickly.

OPERATIONS

Camouflage Barrage operation is carried out by Right Group at 06.00. No success is obtained in attempts to cross the canal. Impression gained by majority now is that enemy is holding East bank of canal very strongly and will continue to do so until our attack towards DENAIN develops further.

ARTILLERY RELIEF

Taking advantage of the lull on the front today CRA decides to interchange the guns of 1st & 3rd Brigades CFA placing these brigades in groups of their own Divisional artilleries. For this interchange 3rd Brigade CFA now in positions near VITRY-EN-ARTOIS and BREBIERES move to vicinity of TORTEQUENNE. From 13.00 to 22.00 these brigades of Field artillery cover Div'l Front while this move is being carried out. At 22.00 hours 4th CDA under CRA 4th Can Div covers the 1st Can Inf Brigade on the Left section. Relief and move is carried out without mishap 3rd Brigade having 4 guns per battery in new positions before 18.00 hours.

SITUATION ON DIVISIONAL FRONT

During the early morning patrols of Left Brigade succeed in crossing canal by cork bridges but are held up by SENSEE river further on. Further south patrols enter FERIN. All patrols withdraw at dawn owing to untenability of position between Canal and SENSEE [river] due to machine gun fire from enemy trenches immediately to the east.

Enemy artillery very active throughout the night but abnormally quiet during day. About noon impression is got by Corps HQs that enemy has withdrawn due to lack of movement in his lines and no N.F. calls reported by Artillery air patrols. This is merely a delusion as is found by investigation.

GENERAL SITUATION

In spite of peace moves, allies attack in BELGIUM and make good progress. German reply to President Wilson's note is reported to be one of acquiescence to all demands. This however, is thought to be only another manoeuvre on part of the Hun to give him time to extract him[self] from his perilous position north and south and withdraw to another line of resistance without being hampered by the allied forces.

The Allied policy continues to be one of not directly attacking the enemy but stimulating their retirement by using artillery to harass every move by day and to carry out area bombardments by night. There is no need to mount a formal attack, as the enemy are being forced to the rear by the pressure of the Allied advance.

LES FOSSES FME/DURY October/15. Rain throughout most of the day.

MOVE OF HQS 1st CDA

Headquarters 1st Canadian Division Artillery moves from LES FOSSES to QUARRY at DURY during morning. Office opened at 10.00 hours at new location. Slight mishap with arrangements for lorry transport causes mess and kits to be delayed until evening.

OPERATION

Usual Camouflage Barrage placed on Right Infantry Brigade Front. Enemy retaliation slightly heavier than usual but soon dies down. This gives required information as to enemy still holding East bank.

POLICY ON THIS FRONT

Policy on this front is not one of attack. Our troops will keep in touch with enemy at all times and take advantage of the slightest weakening in his defence – otherwise we sit quiet and engage all movement by day and harass vigorously by night. A few attempts at pushing across the canal in face of opposition [by] enemy has cost [us] quite heavily, therefore the 1st Can Div policy will be to get across canal with light casualties which operation can only be carried out by an organised assault or if enemy withdraws.

GENERAL

Major General LIPSETT until recently commanding 3rd Canadian Division is buried today at QUEANT. Enemy continues to give ground north and south.

Peace offensive of the Germanic Tribes seems to be having no better luck than their warring factions are having with the war at the present time. All papers seem quite unanimous in the insincerity of the enemy in his reply.

DURY October/16. Rain throughout the morning. Dull without rain during remainder of day.

OPERATION.

At 06.00 Camouflage Creeping Barrages are put down on both 1st and 2nd Canadian Infantry Brigade fronts. Fair retaliation is reported. 5.9 Battery which shelled ESTREES and GOUY intermittently yesterday is active on the forward area.

During the day Artillery Instruction #39 is issued which puts morning barrages on a sounder basis. Instead of two brigades spreading over a whole Infantry Brigade Front, narrow tender spots are selected on which the guns of the group are concentrated.

AMMUNITION

Ammunition supply still remains good. Two ARPs are being used – LECLUSE & SAILLY. Gas shell for 4.5" Howitzers is being brought forward for use on this front as enemy shows no sign of evacuation.

TRENCH MORTAR

One 6" Newton is in action East of GOUY-SOUS-BELLONNE and is being used daily on Eastern approaches to crossing south of FERIN. The enemy knowing that this will be one of our crossing points has machine guns concentrating in this area but shows [discloses] his position when called upon which fact presents good targets for the Trench Mortar.

GENERAL

Attack in BELGIUM is progressing most favorably. Our troops are NE of COURTRAI and hold THOUROUT. If this continues nothing will prevent us reaching the coast to the Dutch Frontier.

The anticipated withdrawal of the enemy north of this sector appears to be taking place. Canadian infantry crosses the Canal de la Sensée following an artillery barrage, but the enemy is very active in delaying the advancing troops, this time thwarting attempts to cross using pontoons by breaking the dyke bank of the canal. Bridges have to be constructed as a result. Artillery is moved up to the canal in order to give close support to the advancing infantry. While the enemy is actively resisting, one can sense that the Germans are beaten and the end is near. Although this is not very obvious to those fully engaged in pursuing them, the plight of the enemy is dire.

DURY October/17. Dull weather.
ENEMY WITHDRAWAL

First reports of enemy withdrawal on a large scale are received about 10.00 hours when it is reported by 5th Army that their troops are in THUMIERES (East of CARVIN) and farther north that LILLE is being evacuated.

A 6-inch Howitzer with gun crew. (*Courtesy of the RCA Museum*)

Practically no movement is seen when the Camouflage Creeping Barrage is put down at FERIN at 06.15. No retaliation results. Our patrols push across the canal into FERIN during the morning and are reported close to or on DOUAI – CAMBRAI road by noon.

Engineers begin pontooning canal but owing to breaking of dyke bank near DOUAI during early morning by enemy, pontoons cannot be used north of lock in K10c south of FERIN. This delays crossing on north as bridges must now be built. First pontoon bridge is ready by 17.00 and two more shortly afterwards.

By nightfall infantry are on line SIN LE NOBLE – DECHY – ROCOURT – Heights SE of CANTIN. This line is being held for the night but patrols are being pushed well forward to seize LEWARD – ERCHIN Heights.

ARTILLERY

At 14.00 hours Groups are ordered to push two batteries per brigade forward to Canal. Remaining batteries to move up as soon as first batteries are on position.

All Btys are in position along canal by 21.00 hours. Right Goup in K16 & K22; Left Group in E26, K2 & 3.

One bty of Left Group goes across canal at 22.00 hours to position of assembly in E21 North East of FERIN.

GENERAL

Reports state that OSTEND, LILLE, ROUBAIX & TOURCOING all occupied by our troops.

DURY/FERIN. October/18. Fair weather but misty.

ENEMY WITHDRAWAL

During early morning our patrols seizing the only remaining height (LEWARD – ERCHIN). Pursuit of enemy continues throughout the day. Our forces are feeling along cautiously and at nightfall are holding general line – western outskirts of PECQUENCOURT and ECAILLON.

Throughout the retirement enemy has continued the destruction of trivial things – sacking of chateaux, burning furniture etc. He has systematically blown up level crossings of railways and main highways over ditches and creeks. These are all obstacles for the moment.

ARTILLERY

The batteries are mainly in Assembly Areas throughout the day. One battery is sent forward with each Front Line Battalion as usual. By dusk batteries are in position in following areas: 1st & 2nd Brigades CFA MONTIGNY – LOFRE; 3rd Brigade CFA FEWARDE; 4th Brigade CFA ERCHIN.

Practically no expenditure of ammunition is made during the day as the [enemy] appears to have evacuated the entire area early today. Shooting promiscuously is not allowed owing to the presence of hundreds of French civilians in the towns and villages being occupied at present.

MOVE OF 1st CDA HQs

HQs 1st CDA moves from DURY to FERIN, a small town south of DOUAI and on Canal de la SENSEE. Owing to rapid advance it is doubtful if locations will be close enough by tomorrow noon.

FERIN/LEWALDE October 19. Very misty weather with drizzling rain at intervals.
ENEMY WITHDRAWAL

Enemy withdrawal continues today. From French civilians in towns occupied this morning it is learned that enemy infantry withdrew yesterday leaving patrols and cavalry to blow up road crossings at the last moment. Enemy cavalry clear from WANDIGNIES – HORNAING Area about noon closely followed by our cavalry and cyclists.

3rd Canadian Infantry Brigade passes through 2nd Canadian Infantry Brigade in early morning: the latter passing to Divisional Reserve.

Most forward line reached by our patrols is immediately west of BOIS DES ECLUSETTES east of BOIS ST AMAND and east of HELESMES.

All towns captured today are occupied by French civilians – women, children and old men. They are almost frenzied with joy when welcoming our troops – rushing out into the streets and throwing themselves on the necks of the surprised Tommies and gunners.

ARTILLERY RELIEF

In the very early morning orders are received for the withdrawal of 3rd Brigade CFA (4th Canadian Division Artillery) before dawn and the relief later in the day of the 4th Brigade CFA (4th CDA) by the 8th Army Brigade CFA. Owing to the great extent of the advance today the latter relief is not carried out before midnight 19/20th as the 8th Army Brigade CFA could not overtake the 4th Brigade CFA who had orders to continue the support of the infantry until actually relieved.

ARTILLERY POSITION

By nightfall artillery are in position approximately as follows: 1st and 2nd Brigades CFA supporting Left Inf Brigade in area near WANDIGNIES – HAMAGE; 4th Brigade CFA supporting Right Inf Brigade in HORNAING Area.

LEWALDE October/20. Dull and misty with rain.

ENEMY WITHDRAWAL

Enemy does not intend to be hurried in his withdrawal. Today machine guns and 77s, 4.1s were scattered about area of our advance. Due to mist it is found difficult to locate them quickly and the result is apparent as our line is advanced only about 3000 – 5000 yards.

Enemy shells villages of WALLERS, CATAINE and HASNOIT in spite of their being full of civilians.

ARTILLERY

8th Army Brigade arrive in forward area in time to begin the advance in the morning. 4th Brigade CFA are seen marching to 4th Canadian Division Area about noon. Canadian Corps advise that only one brigade of Field Artillery will advance in support of each infantry brigade. 2nd Brigade CFA [is] ordered to remain in WANDIGNIES Area owing to the fact that Lt Col

A 9.2-inch Howitzer limbered up. (*Courtesy of the RCA Museum*)

Anderson is proceeding on leave. Artillery in support will be Right Infantry Brigade – 8th Army Brigade CFA Left Infantry Brigade – 1st Brigade CFA.

GENERAL

It is not considered that enemy intends to hold his present line. Explosions are being reported in VALENCIENNES direction. Further withdrawal will probably be made tomorrow.

LEWARDE/MASNY October/21. Dull with intermittent drizzle. [Temp BM writes].

HQ 1st CDA moves in the morning [to] MASNY – making room in LEWARDE for Can Corps HQ.

ENEMY WITHDRAWAL

During the night 20/21st enemy resistance again weakened and in the morning our patrols advance.

Major A H Bick Brigade Major proceeds on leave, Capt H H Blake RO assuming his duties [writes these diaries] during his absence.

The 1st Canadian Division is in the process of being relieved, having been in continuous action for a considerable time on this front. The 2nd, 3rd and 4th Canadian Divisions will take over the pursuit of the enemy and also deal with the heavily defended and strongly disputed Mont Houy outside Valenciennes.

MASNY October 22. Misty and drizzling during morning – dull but clear in afternoon.
RELIEF

During the morning, 3rd Canadian Division passed through 1st Canadian Division – 9th Brigade CFA relieving 1st Brigade CFA and 10th Brigade CFA relieving 8th Brigade CFA – CRA 3rd Canadian Division assumed command at 12.00.

DISPOSITIONS

On completion of relief 1st CDA units were disposed as follows: 1st Brigade CFA – GRAND BRAY; 2nd Brigade CFA – WANDIGNIES HAMAGE; 1st CDAC – HORNAING; 1st Canadian Division Trench Mortar Brigade ERRE. All units have good billets, the french civilians being most obliging, but horse standings are in open and very muddy.

During morning, CRA visited 2nd Brigade CFA. The horses found to be in good shape generally considering the hard and continuous work they have been having lately.

Brigades carrying out training and reorganisation.

MASNY October/23. Fine night – misty in morning, becoming fine – no rain.

During morning CRA visited 1st Brigade. Horses thin but should pick up during present period of rest.

Brigade continue training and reorganisation.

Capt R O BENNETT, Staff Capt and Capt J E GENET Sig Officer return from leave.

MASNY October/24. Fine day – resulting in considerable improvement to roads.

MASNY/ HERMITAGE CHATEAU October/25. Cloudy day with some drizzle.

HQs 1st CDA moves to HERMITAGE CHATEAU (T24b Sheet 51A) apparently practically no looting had been done here by the BOSCHE and the whole place with its contents has been carefully kept.

The Corps Commander [General A. W. Currie] pays a visit and stays to lunch.

Brigades continue training and reorganisation.

HERMITAGE CHATEAU October/26. Fine day with early morning mist.

During morning CRA visits 2nd Brigade CFA. Horses beginning to pick up with the abundance of forage in the area and good opportunities for grazing.

During afternoon the CRA and Divisional Commander visited 2nd Brigade CFA and with ADVS and DADVS [Veterinary Officers] inspected a batch of newly arrived remounts – a poor lot – GOC also inspected batteries of 2nd Brigade CFA.

During the latter stages of the war, it became increasingly difficult to provide enough good quality horses to replace casualties.

HERMITAGE CHATEAU October/27. Fine day.

During morning CRA visited 1st Brigade CFA inspecting 3rd and 4th Batteries.

Brigades continue training.

HERMITAGE CHATEAU October/28. Fine day.

During morning CRA visited 1st Brigade CFA inspecting 1st and 2nd Batteries.

Brigades continue training.

HERMITAGE CHATEAU October/29. Cloudy in morning – fine in afternoon.

During morning CRA visited 1st CDAC and 1st CDTM Brigade and in afternoon 2nd Brigade CFA.

HERMITAGE CHATEAU October/30. Fine and cool.

CRA visited 1st Brigade CFA in the morning. Brigades continue training.

HERMITAGE CHATEAU October/31. Mostly fine in morning – drizzle in afternoon.

Brigades continue training.

The cessation of nocturnal visitations by enemy bombing planes has been a most welcome feature of the latter half of the month.

News received that hostilities ceased with TURKEY at noon yesterday.

Diaries for November 1918

The 1st Canadian Divisional Artillery remained in reserve while the rest of the Canadian Corps pressed the retiring enemy. At Mont Houy outside Valenciennes, the Germans took advantage of the flooded terrain where this feature dominated the only entry to the town. Here the Germans made an attempt to stem the Canadian advance but were rapidly overcome by artillery fire; the Canadians occupied Valenciennes to the great joy of its inhabitants. Despite the fact that it was known that Germany was seeking terms for an armistice, their troops continued their fighting retreat, always contesting the ground before leaving it to the advancing allies. In the south of the Western Front, the American Corps were winning their first engagements around St Mihiel, and the French were also successful nearby. There was a feeling of imminent victory among the Allied High Command.

L'HERMITAGE CHATEAU November/1. Dull with bright intervals.

Brigades continue training. News received of Austria signing armistice with Italy.

L'HERMITAGE CHATEAU November/2. Dull with intermittent drizzle.

In the morning Divisional Commander accompanied by CRA inspects horses of 1st Brigade CFA. He impresses on BCs the importance of good stable management,

4th Canadian Division complete capture of VALENCIENNES.

L'HERMITAGE CHATEAU November/3. Mostly fine – occasional drizzle.

During morning enemy commences to withdraw on Canadian Corps Front.

L'HERMITAGE CHATEAU November/4. Fine

Brigades continue training. 2 Musketry, 1 Lewis gun and 1 gymnastic instructors arrive from Divisional wing and are distributed amongst brigades and DAC. GOC 1st Canadian Division proceeds to England on special leave and CRA assumes command of the Division.

1st CDA moves into readiness again to give support to the other Canadian artillery groups who have been engaged for some considerable time.

L'HERMITAGE CHATEAU November/5. Continual drizzle all day.

During the morning orders are received from RA Canadian Corps for the 1st CDA to move to the ANZIN – ST WAAST LA HAUT – AUBRY Area on November 6th. It is anticipated that Brigades will shortly reinforce the line on 3rd Canadian Division Front.

L'HERMITAGE CHATEAU November/6. Continual drizzle all day.
MARCH

1st CDA moved from present billets at 09.00 to ANZIN – AUBRY Area and are located as follows: 1st Brigade CFA, ANZIN; 2nd Brigade CFA, ST WAAST LA HAUT; 1st CDAC AUBRY; 1st CDTM Brigade, ANZIN. Roads and conditions for marching are very bad.

Orders are received from RA Canadian Corps that 1st CDA will be transferred from Corps Reserve to 3rd Canadian Division at 12.00 November 7th and be prepared to relieve Army Brigades under 3rd CDA.

CRA attends Demobilisation Conference at Canadian Corps HQs in the morning.

L'HERMITAGE CHATEAU/VALENCIENNES November/7. Dull with intermittent drizzle.
MARCH

During morning 1st CDA units march to following locations: 1st Brigade CFA, ST SAULVE; 2nd Brigade CFA, ONNAING; 1st CDAC, E4c Northern outskirts of VALENCIENNES; 1st CDTM Brigade E10a North outskirts of VALENCIENNES; HQ 1st CDA to VALENCIENNES.

RELIEF

During afternoon 2nd Brigade CFA relieves 126th Army Brigade RFA under 3rd CDA and occupies positions in vicinity of CRESPIN in support of 8th Canadian Infantry Brigade.

ENEMY WITHDRAWAL

Enemy continues to withdraw on Canadian Corps Front under cover of rearguard. 3rd Canadian Division form defensive flank along MONS CANAL – the 8th Canadian Infantry Brigade going into the line on afternoon November 7th for this purpose.

By dusk following approximate line occupied by 3rd Canadian Division patrols; N32b – N26a – N19a – N10a thence west along MONS CANAL.

GENERAL

News is received that 4 German plenipotentiaries left Germany on November 6th to conclude terms of armistice with Marshal Foch. Any troops seeing a party with white flag to send them to Divisional HQ and thence to GHQ.

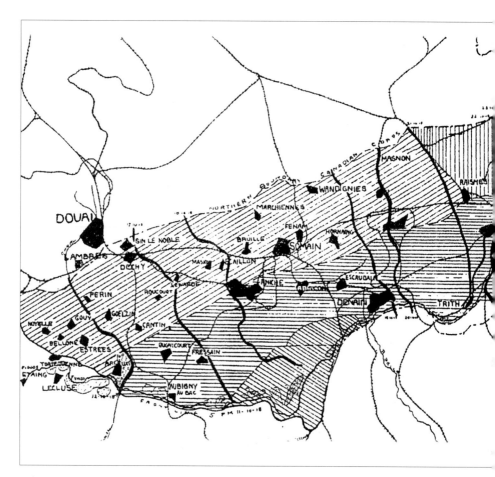

Advances made by the Canadian Corps from 11 October to 11 November 1918.

VALENCIENNES November/8. [Major A. H. Bick returns to write diary] Fair weather.

Reports of arrival of plenipotentiaries received – also that Foch has given 72 hours for their acceptance.

Officer patrols sent out by 2nd Brigade CFA encounter heavy machine gun fire from vicinity of canal North and North East of CRISPIN. 2nd Brigade Batteries are all in action South of CRISPIN along road.

Although the end is clearly in sight, artillery support is needed to maintain pressure on the enemy. Furthermore, the Canadian infantry presses on to occupy Mons.

VALENCIENNES November/9. Rain throughout most of the day.

Warning is received verbally from GOCRA that operation may be carried out by two Divisional Artilleries (1st and 5th) from Canal in vicinity of

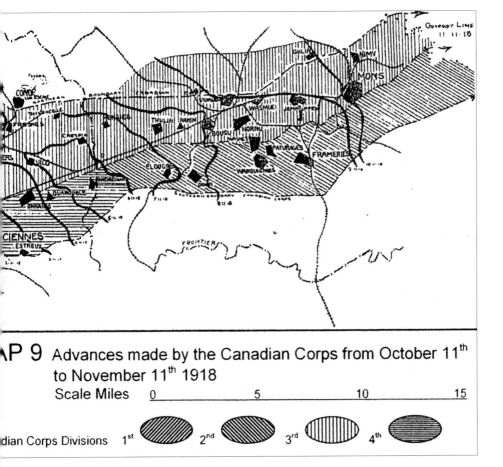

AP 9 Advances made by the Canadian Corps from October 11th to November 11th 1918

Scale Miles 0   5   10   15

dian Corps Divisions   1st   2nd   3rd   4th

CRISPIN Northwards. This may necessitate gun dumps of 600 rounds. Later in the day reports give enemy retiring in haste from this portion of the line. 1st Brigade CFA has however completed a reconnaissance of positions for this operation previous to the arrival of these reports.

1st Brigade billets are very poor. Endeavors to change things meet with no success.

Everyone is waiting with great expectancy the Hun reply to Foch's armistice terms. It is felt that the enemy cannot but accept them. Northern Germany is now reported in hands of revolutionary party and all communication between BERLIN and naval bases is down.

At 21.00 o'clock word is received from 3rd CDA that 2nd Brigade CFA is ordered to withdraw to wagon lines forthwith. 1st CDA comes into Corps Reserve.

VALENCIENNES November/10. Fine weather but turning to rain at night.

All ranks await reply to our terms for armistice.

The Canadians, having cleared Mons before 6 a.m., press on beyond in order to keep pressure on the enemy and consolidate their position. When the Armistice comes into effect at 6.30 a.m., they are several miles east of Mons itself. However, there appears to be some confusion as it is understood in 1st CDA that 11 a.m. is the time when the Armistice is to take effect. In fact there is little resistance by the enemy later that morning although suspicions of their true intent persist and the front line is maintained in a state of high alert.

VALENCIENNES November/11. Fine weather.

In early morning word is received that armistice will take effect at 11.00. Enemy has agreed to all our terms. Line is being pressed forward until hour at which hostilities cease.

Demonstration takes place in MONS (captured at dawn this morning) at 11.00. Civilians are delirious with joy at the release and can hardly believe that peace is in sight.

CRA proceeds on leave to England during afternoon.

Rumors are going about that 2nd and 4th Armies will march to RHINE and remaining armies stay where they are now. Canadian Corps is being transferred to 2nd Army.

The advances made by the Canadian Corps from 11 October to 11 November 1918, when the terms of the Armistice took effect, are shown in Map 9.

CHAPTER EIGHT

Marching to the Rhine

A Long Walk and an Occupation with a Defended Perimeter, 12 November 1918 – 18 January 1919

The hostilities over, a sense of anticlimax set in. After such intense activity and exposure to extreme danger to life and limb, the lack of a clear objective was particularly difficult to deal with. The feeling of exhilaration having won the last battles of the long war quickly gave way to exhaustion and frustration. Planning for demobilisation and return to Canada seemed uncertain. Policy about the arrangements for transport home was an issue that finally required General Currie's intervention. He insisted that arrangements best suited to the Canadians – repatriation by fighting units – should be adopted. Morale dropped when it appeared that the troops were powerless in their present situation. Discipline began to be a problem as a result of idleness and boredom, and it took some ingenious initiatives by commanders to combat these aspects of post-war life in the army.

The 1st and 2nd Canadian Divisions were selected to join the occupation force and preparations had to be made for a long march to the German border through the German-speaking region of Belgium, where the inhabitants were increasingly apathetic. In Germany the people were polite but not particularly cooperative and until the currency exchange rate was agreed, costs of food and supplies were exorbitant. The advance was to be along the same roads that the Germans used to evacuate their forces. The roads were in very poor condition as a result of this heavy traffic. Furthermore, a decent interval needed to be left to allow the Germans to retire. This was a welcome break because bulk supplies of food, particularly for the horses, had to be brought up from depots a long way back.

Billets in Germany were in barracks where conditions were quite comfortable. However, a defensive perimeter needed to be maintained because of the unrest among both the civilian population and the enemy military who were awaiting demobilisation. Some appeared likely to attempt a resistance movement.

In December 1918, the first peaceful Christmas and New Year for four years was celebrated. The occupation was the final act of the Canadian Corps in its military capacity. Plans were made to withdraw to Belgium and prepare for demobilisation later in January.

------oOo------

Diaries for 12 November Onwards

VALENCIENNES November/12. Fair weather.

All ranks are awaiting word as to their next task – whether it will be salving a certain area, marching east as part of army of occupation, or proceeding back to Canada.

Orders are being issued to have everything smartened up and cleaned up as much as possible.

VALENCIENNES November/13. Dull and slightly misty.

Preparations being made for move during the next few days.

VALENCIENNES/JEMAPPES November/14. Dull and slight drizzle.

Divisional Artillery HQs and Divisional HQs move to JEMAPPES. All units are preparing for move tomorrow.

JEMAPPES November/15. Fair weather with slight mist.

Units move during afternoon to WASMES Area. 1st Brigade CFA and 1st CDTM Brigade to BOUSSU, 2nd Brigade CFA to THULIN, 1st CDAC to HAININ. Accommodation in new billets is not very ample.

The 1st and 2nd Divisions of the Canadian Corps will march to the Rhine as part of the 2nd Army, a distance of over 160 miles. It will be at least 100 miles through liberated Belgian countryside and a further 60 miles as unwelcome conquerors through German territory. It will be a test not only of the logistical arrangements to keep them supplied with food and clean clothing, but also a new kind of challenge after three years of fighting.

JEMAPPES November/16. Dull weather with heavy mists.

Preparations now being completed for the march to the Rhine. 14th Brigade CFA and one section 5th CDAC will march with 1st CDA.

It is decided to form three infantry brigade groups – each group complete with its own artillery, engineers etc. Each group will have 1 brigade CFA with one section DAC.

JEMAPPES November/17. Misty.

Certain units move east so that they will be better placed to commence marching tomorrow.

Canadian Corps Orders decide the breaking up of the Trench Mortar Brigades. The personnel to be divided up amongst units of Divisional Artillery. It seems very regrettable that a unit which has had a fighting record such as the 1st CDTM Brigade should be broken up now that the war is over and not allowed to go back to Canada as a unit.

The long march begins in cold, unpleasant weather. However, the troops are greeted everywhere by delighted and enthusiastic inhabitants who have suffered occupation for the past four years. Although this is a triumphant progress, they cannot delay very much to enjoy the benefits of their welcome.

JEMAPPES/NEUFVILLE November/18. Dull with rain.

March is being carried on satisfactorily. Divisional Artillery HQs moves to NEUFVILLE.

NEUFVILLE November/19. Misty.

Lieut Col J G PIERCEY DSO died yesterday in #6 Casualty Clearing Station. Word has not been received as to cause.

NEUFVILLE November/20. Cool, fair weather.

Billetting parties go forward to NIVELLES Area to arrange about billets for tomorrows move.

Captain H H BLAKE and Lieut D F PEPLER are evacuated to hospital suffering from effects of influenza.

Owing to distance away of our units and the state of the roads no visit is paid to brigades. Car situation is still serious – no sign of a car to replace one damaged at Boulogne on 11th inst.

It is necessary to delay the journey in order for supplies to be brought up particularly for the horses but also food for the men. It is a long and testing march for everyone especially after all the effort of fighting. However, being part of a victorious army ensures that morale is high.

NEUFVILLE/NIVELLE November/21. Cool, signs of rain towards evening.

6-inch Howitzers returning from the lines. (*F. Wade Moses, Montreal, courtesy of the RCA Museum*)

HQs 1st CDA moves with Divisional Headquarters to NIVELLES. Civic reception given Canadians who are acclaimed as liberators of Belgium by the Burgomaster of NIVELLES.

Dumps of guns and aeroplanes lie on outskirts of the town. Apparently the Belgian civilians gave the German guards considerable cause for worry for their lives as British guards had to be mounted to protect German guards.

NIVELLE November/22. Fair weather. Frosty at night.

Civilian population continues its celebration of deliverance.

NIVELLE November/23. Frosty with fine weather.

Conference of all General Officers and Commanders at Corps HQs MONS held to deal with question of unrest amongst the troops now that hostilities have ceased. All artillery commanders point out that there wasn't any sign of unrest amongst artillerymen of the Corps. This is probably due to an artilleryman's time being taken up by certain necessary duties such as grooming horses, cleaning vehicles [etc]. Any spare time he usually uses to better advantage than concocting organized schemes for disturbance.

"D" Group 1st Canadian Division under command of Lieut Colonel PENHALE DSO and comprising HQs details of Division and #3 Section and HQs 1st CDAC move to BAULERS NE of NIVELLE during the day.

NIVELLE November/24. Frosty.

GOC 1st Canadian Division visits WATERLOO Battlefield in company with CRA, CRE and GSO1. Party afterwards proceeds to BRUSSELS for the afternoon.

Orders for move tomorrow are received. Grouping of Divisional Units remains the same.

NIVELLE/GEMBLOUX November/25. Dull weather. Roads very muddy. Slight rain towards evening.

HQs 1st CDA moves during day to GEMBLOUX on road between BRUSSELS and NAMUR.

Park of about 60 German guns is found in field behind HQs billets. All Bosche guns seen up to date are in frightfully dirty condition. No sights or gun stores are being left with guns.

CRA visits 1st Brigade CFA at CORROY LE CHATEAU and finds billets quite fair.

GEMBLOUX November/26. Dull with rain.

CRA visits 14th Brigade CFA at VILLERS LA VILLE and 2nd Brigade CFA at SAUVENIERES. 2nd Brigade report considerable trouble re billets with 29th Division on left. This is adjusted satisfactorily to all concerned with help of Divisional Staff Officers.

GEMBLOUX/BEN AHIN November/27. Dull with drizzling rain.

HQs 1st CDA moves to BEN AHIN near HUY and on road between NAMUR and LIÈGE. Owing to great distance of this move transport stages for the night NE of NAMUR.

BEN AHIN November/28. Dull with rain at intervals throughout the day.

HQs transport arrives at BEN AHIN.

Motor car in replacement of the one destroyed near BOULOGNE on 11th inst arrives but is not considered to be of much value. This is the car supplied during the past year which on arrival would appear to last a month of hard driving.

Warning received that move to OCHAIN Chateau will be carried out tomorrow.

BEN AHIN November/29. Frosty. Roads in good condition and hard.

No move is being carried out today by any Divisional Troops due to non-arrival of rations. Rations for today's consumption arrive at forward group about 15.00 hours. If situation does not improve no move is possible tomorrow.

Word is received that for political reasons it is most necessary that advanced troops arrive at frontier on night 2nd December. Everything now depends on supply of rations.

BEN AHIN/PONCHON November/30. Frosty weather. Slightly misty.

HQs 1st CDA moves to Chateau at PONCHON east of OCHAIN where 1st Canadian Division HQs is established. Billets and accommodation for whole HQs is good.

Brigadier General H C THACKER CMG DSO arrives back from English leave after a two day trip from BOULOGNE and relieves Lieut Colonel ANDERSON of duties of CRA.

Diaries for December 1918

The nearest railhead was at Valencienne; therefore supplies had to be brought up by lorry. As the troops advanced towards the Rhine, this journey took longer and longer. Sometimes lorries broke down and supplies reached the troops on the morning of the march, resulting in frequent delays of more than a day. In the inclement weather it was particularly important to ensure that the horses, the only means of moving equipment in the line of march and providing personal mobility, were well supplied with oats to stop their condition deteriorating rapidly. In addition to these delays, stops were made to ensure that the retiring German formations were well clear. However, these delays were not unwelcome because rests were essential for the troops who would find marching every day on this long journey very hard indeed.

PONCHON CHATEAU December/1. Frosty and clear.

Owing to non-arrival of rations no move is taking place; all units of the Division remaining in billets occupied last night. Unless Ration situation takes a rapid improvement Divisional Artillery will be practically immobile. Ration lorry carrying oats for today's consumption for 1st Brigade CFA breaks down en route during afternoon thereby necessitating requisitioning of oats by OC 1st Brigade CFA.

Transport of 1st CDA HQs moves to MY about 25 Kms distance.

PONCHON CHATEAU/GRAND HALLEUX December/2. Cool and misty.

HQs 1st CDA moves to GRAND HALLEUX about 6 Kms West of German Frontier. Transport of HQs remains for the day at MY.

All units are on the move today. Roads traversed by leading Group are very hilly and muddy – on one place East of WERBOMONT there is a gradual rise of about 250 metres in 5 Kms.

Bad condition of roads is said by civilians to be due to the fact that German transport passed by this route continuously for 15 days prior to the arrival of allied army.

GRAND HALLEUX December/3. Rain and fairly misty.

CRA proceeded to vicinity of LIENNEUX and intercepted 1st Brigade CFA en route to LIENNEUX. Major McMURTRY OC 1st Brigade CFA reports ration situation becoming serious again. All batteries appeared in good shape and men in good spirits in spite of rain.

GRAND HALLEUX December/4. Rain and misty.

CRA intercepts 2nd Brigade CFA West of BASSE BODEUX. Ration situation in this brigade is very serious. March is of 40 Kms and over bad roads and without rations. No march is possible for this brigade tomorrow unless horses are to be sacrificed.

GRAND HALLEUX December/5. Rain.

Owing to Ration shortage no move of artillery units is made from points reached last night. Two Rations begin to arrive in afternoon and preparations are being made for move tomorrow.

Major C V STOCKWELL DSO and Major H T C WHITLEY arrive from Reserve Artillery Depot in England and proceed to 1st Brigade CFA pending posting.

Crossing the border into German territory is undramatic, but it is unsurprising that the local people seem indifferent and unforthcoming. Rates of exchange, important when making local purchases, appear to be very expensive when changing centimes for deutschmarks.

GRAND HALLEUX/LIGNEUVILLE December/6. Dull with rain at intervals.

HQs 1st CDA moves to LIGNEUVILLE about 5 Kms inside Germany territory. Inhabitants in this district appear to be mostly of French extraction although several true Huns are encountered.

Some difficulty exists over prices to be paid for various commodities. Prices demanded are much too great. Orders are received that German mark is valued officially at 70 centimes which helps the situation considerably.

LIGNEUVILLE December/7. Fair during morning but turning to rain at dusk.

CRA inspects 14th Brigade CFA west of RECHT during morning. This brigade hasn't suffered to any extent from ration shortage. Men appear to be in good spirits.

All artillery units move during the day. 1st Brigade to CFA to REIFFERSHIED, 2nd Brigade CFA to KRINKELT, 14th Brigade CFA to RECHT and 1st CDA HQs and #3 section to VIELSALM.

LIGNEUVILLE/HELLENTHAUL December/8. Dull and Misty.

HQs 1st CDA moves to an Hotel in HELLENTHAUL.

HELLENTHAUL/EUSKIRCHEN December/9. Dull and slightly misty with rain towards evening.

HQs moves to EUSKIRCHEN. Billets are quite fair.

CRA inspects 2nd Brigade CFA on road east of KALL. Spirits of men appear to be improving as FORET DES ARDENNES Country is being left behind. Roads in area passed through by two leading brigades are quite passable.

EUSKIRCHEN December/10. Weather appears to be improving.

It seems now possible that entire 1st Canadian Division will cross the Rhine and not only two brigades as was formerly thought likely. There apparently will be an outpost line and main defence line. Trenches will be dug and guns placed in position. Crossing of the Rhine is set now for 13th but may possibly be later.

"A" Group reaches bank of Rhine today and occupies area of concentration assigned by Division. Each successive day will bring another group into this area.

General attitude of population is not one of great hostility in this area. Treatment in billets is quite good and much better than in many areas occupied during past four years.

EUSKIRCHEN/BRÜHL December/11. Fine weather; still muddy underfoot; heavy rain towards evening.

HQ moves to BRÜHL about seven miles SW of COLOGNE. District now being occupied appears quite rich. Houses are generally large and well furnished. Supply of food is not small apparently judging from appearance of civilians.

2nd Brigade CFA moves into concentration area along Rhine between COLOGNE and BONN. 14th Brigade CFA arrives in the area tomorrow thereby completing the arrivals of artillery brigades in Divisional Concentration Area.

BRÜHL December/12. Dull with rain.

1st and 2nd Brigades CFA remain in billets today and prepare for march through COLOGNE tomorrow. 14th Brigade CFA moves during the day to suburb of COLOGNE and will be the first artillery brigade to cross the Rhine tomorrow.

Plans for the holding of the bridgehead are now being worked out at "G" Branch 1st Canadian Division. Artillery will probably pass to control of CRA about 14th December if Ration transfers can be effected.

BRÜHL December/13. Rain.

GOC 1st Canadian Division with his staff and CRA ride through COLOGNE at head of 1st Divisional Troops. Crossing of the south bridge begins at 09.30 coincident with crossing of the north bridge by 29th (British) Division. GOC remains at saluting point at bridge while entire Division marches by. During later portion of march past General PLUMER, 2nd British Army Commander takes the salute.

It is remarked by all the good condition of all units. This is confirmed later by a message of commendation from GOC.

BRÜHL December/14. Dull weather.

Artillery units move to billets which it is hoped will be occupied permanently while in this area. 1st Brigade – WAHN; 2nd Brigade – EIL; 14th Brigade – OSTREIM; 1st CDAC – WESTHOVEN. 2nd and 14th Brigades CFA will have one battery forward with outpost line.

Brigades are warned to make reconnaissance of forward area with a view to going into action to cover an arbitrary line of defence along the AGGAR River. Later it is reported that RA Canadian Corps will lay down artillery policy.

BRÜHL/COLOGNE December/15. Dull weather.

CRA proceeds to forward area and makes reconnaissance of area along Main line of Defence. Country is not so rough as would appear from details on the map.

HQs 1st CDA moves to suburb on south edge of COLOGNE. Quarters are very good.

COLOGNE December/16. Dull weather.

GOC, CRA and staffs meet Sir Douglas Haig at church in DEUTZ at 11.30 hours. Our C in C is reported to be about to proceed back to England. He apparently wishes to say goodbye to as many of the various staffs as he can.

CRA visits 1st CDAC at WESTHOVEN. Arrangements are being made by Lieut Colonel PENHALE to have the whole DAC Group collected in WESTHOVEN Area.

COLOGNE December/17. Misty with rain at intervals.

Reconnaissance of area on 2nd Brigade Front in vicinity of MARIALINDEN is carried out by CRA. Practically any line of Defence in this area can be covered without much difficulty. A Defence Line must first be decided on then positions can be selected. As yet only rough areas are located.

COLOGNE December/18. Misty with showers [Capt. H. H. Blake writes the diary]

CRA visited HQs 1st, 2nd and 14th Brigades reference educational scheme.

COLOGNE December/19. Alternate snow, sleet and rain.

CRA held conference of unit Education Officers at 2nd Brigade HQs. The scheme of Education was explained by Lieut Wilson Divisional Education Officer

Lt Colonel COSGROVE, reporting as OC 1st Brigade was taken to 1st Brigade HQs by CRA.

COLOGNE December/20. Dull and misty in morning becoming fine later.

CRA made reconnaissance of 1st Brigade area visiting GEBER and SCHEIDERHÖHE.

COLOGNE December/21. Dull with rain at intervals.

Major A H Bick proceeds on leave, his duties being assumed by Capt H H Blake.

COLOGNE December/22. Fine.

CRA attended Memorial Service of 1st Brigade CFA at WAHN and afterwards visited 1st, 2nd and 14th Brigade HQs and 1st CDAC distributing educational books.

COLOGNE December/23. Fine morning; rainy afternoon.

"Principles of Defence of COLOGNE bridgehead" received from 1st Canadian Division. Brigades were instructed to make a thorough reconnaissance of their areas and draw up Defence schemes.

COLOGNE December/24. Fine.

COLOGNE December/25. Dull cold day with some snow en early morning.

During morning CRA visited 1st, 2nd and 14th Brigade's HQs and 1st CDAC.

During the last year of the war, the post-war education of serving soldiers was anticipated by the formation of the Khaki University of Canada. Preparation for entry to their courses could now begin with lectures held for individual units. Later, suitable students would be entered for matriculation courses leading in some cases to the first two years of a university arts course. Furthermore, soldiers who had already attended universities in Canada for at least two years prior to enlisting were offered places at universities in Great Britain. Major Bick, having attended Queen's University, Kingston, for several years prior to his enlistment, opted to finish his course at a university in England.

COLOGNE December/26. Dull cold day.

Educational books were delivered to units.

COLOGNE December/27. Misty and showery; milder.

CRA visited 14th Brigade HQs regarding positions selected for batteries for defence of Main Line of Resistance.

COLOGNE is placed out of bounds to all officers and ORs.

Staff Captain accompanies ADVs and DADVs Canadian Corps in an inspection of horses which proved very satisfactory.

The German population was becoming very unsettled in the period following the Armistice. Furthermore, it could not be assumed that some members of the former fighting units would not attempt to disrupt or even attack the occupying garrisons established in German territory. For this reason, schemes were drawn up to create a defensive perimeter to deter such elements and take action against them should the need arise.

COLOGNE December/28. Misty and showery.

During morning CRA visited all Brigade HQs and 1st CDAC regarding discipline.

Warning order received from 1st Canadian Division to the effect that the 1st Canadian Division would be relieved early January and transferred to Fourth Army. Orders sent to units to complete Defence schemes as quickly as possible.

COLOGNE December/29. Misty and showery.

COLOGNE December/30. Fine with some showers.

Major J D HICKMAN proceeded on leave to England.

COLOGNE December/31. Dull and showery.

1st CDA Defence Scheme for Defence of COLOGNE Bridgehead completed and issued.

CRA and staff attended the annual New Year's dinner of 1st Brigade CFA.

Diaries for January 1919

COLOGNE January/1. Cloudy.

During the morning CRA visited 1st and 2nd Brigades HQs.

COLOGNE January/2. Fine.

COLOGNE January/3. Cloudy; light showers.

COLOGNE January/4. Cloudy.

In his absence on leave, it is reported that Major A. H. Bick was awarded the Distinguished Service Order. In July 1918 he had been awarded the

Belgian Croix de Guerre by King Albert I, King of the Belgians. It is most likely that at the same ceremony he was awarded the Order of Leopold II by the King. However, it has been impossible to trace the circumstances or the reason for his being given this latter award. Only two officers of the Canadian Artillery are known to have received this honour.

New Years Honours List received. Major A H Bick awarded DSO – Much satisfaction over award of KCB to Major General A C Macdonell.

Divisional Commander, Unit and Battery commanders dine with CRA.

COLOGNE January/5. Fine.

CRA visits 5th CDA BONN

COLOGNE January/6. Fine.

COLOGNE January/7. Fair.

Major A H BICK DSO returns from leave.

COLOGNE January/8 Fair and warmer [Major A. H. BICK resumes writing diary]

Present indications point to relief of 1st Canadian Division not being completed until 18th or 20th. Divisional Artillery will probably begin to move on 13th.

COLOGNE January/9. Fair but turning to rain later in the day.

Move of the Division is being carried out with three trains per day. Trains from all reports are making good time from here to frontier but beyond the usual uncertainty as to times of arrival begins.

No arrivals yet of 41st Division Artillery advance parties.

RA Canadian Corps report that Canadian Corps "Q" is issuing orders that ammunition will be dumped in present billets and handed over to incoming units. It is unknown as yet whether 41st Division Artillery will leave ammunition in HUY area.

COLOGNE January/10. Rain.

Officer from 41st DAC arrives. Reports that HUY area is not particularly good for billeting.

Orders for entraining of Divisional Artillery arrive from Division. Move will extend from 13th to 18th January. No word yet received of Billets in HUY area. Presumably the artillery will be located in area NW HUY.

COLOGNE January/11. Very dull weather.

Captain LEISHMAN MC 1st Brigade CFA will proceed to new area tomorrow to arrange billets for the artillery.

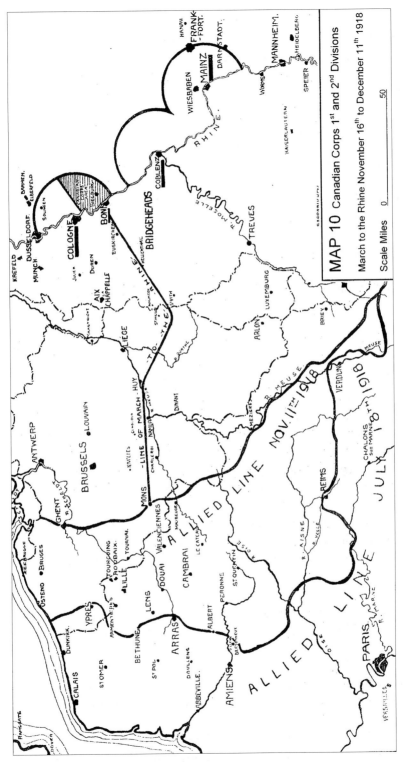

March to the Rhine, 16 November to 11 December 1918.

COLOGNE January/12. Dull weather.

Arrangements for entraining are completed. Artillery will use three trains daily [at] 14.00, 16.00 and 18.00 hours from WAHN station. Facilities for entraining at this point are quite good.

Divisional HQs move to HUY. 1st Canadian Division Artillery come [under] orders [of] 41st Division until completion of relief.

COLOGNE January/13. Fair with rain towards night.

HQs 1st Brigade CFA, 1st and 2nd Batteries CFA and #1 section 1st CDAC move by train to new area. Entraining is carried out quite satisfactorily.

COLOGNE January/14. Dull weather.

Accommodation for officers on trains is very unsatisfactory. Officers of 4th Battery CFA use box car in preference to 3rd Class Coach with broken windows. It seems ridiculous on the face of it that British senior officers should have to ride in such coaches when in the same station Huns are using good 1st Class Coaches to ride to COLOGNE. Special report on this subject is forward[ed] [to] Canadian Corps.

COLOGNE January/15. Rain.

Three batteries 2nd Brigade CFA move by train without incident. Journey is taking from 12 to 15 hours.

COLOGNE January/16. Fine weather.

Traffic [office] 2nd Army at COLOGNE visited regarding condition of Officers accommodation on trains. Promised to better conditions at once.

All trains are reported to be travelling to HUY in good time.

COLOGNE January/17. Rain.

Usual three trains leave WAHN.

CRA travels to BONN to visit Majors WHITLEY and HARDING who are in Casualty Clearing Station. Finds both leaving for the base.

COLOGNE/HUY January/18. Dull and cold.

HQs 1st CDA entrain on 2nd last train for HUY area.

CRA makes trip to HUY by car; remaining for the night in town of HUY.

The line of march and the zones of occupation beyond the Rhine are shown in Map 10.

Their planned return westwards took them through Belgium where, at Liège, the Canadian Corps would parade for the last time before demobilisation.

CHAPTER NINE

Victory Parade in Liège and Demobilisation

Waiting To Go Home Again, 19 January – 15 February 1919

Their last military commitment having been completed, the Canadian Corps returned westwards into Belgium for a triumphant welcome. They were celebrated with a grand parade and reception in Liège, where the town entertained them with parties and dances for all ranks. But it was also a time of sadness because the great comradeship they had experienced during the war was about to come to an end with demobilisation. Furthermore, everyone had to wait to be shipped back to Canada via England. There was a great shortage of shipping due to the demand to return well over a million men, including the US forces, back across the Atlantic. Therefore, the initial stage of the return of the Canadian Corps was via England where they had to stay in specially prepared camps to await their turn to embark for Canada. Most were able to return home within five months. However, some thousands remained in camps in England until the autumn of 1919 and their increasing frustration and anger at this situation can be easily understood.

------oOo------

Diaries for 19 January Onwards

HUY/OTEPPE January/19. Dull weather.
   Brigades visited. Billets are not very good. Several moves have been made since arriving in this area. Batteries are all very much scattered.
   HQs established at CHATEAU D'OTEPPE about 13 Kms NW [of] HUY.

OTEPPE January/20. Rain.

CRA visits several batteries to investigate condition of billets and to see if area presents possibility of bettering them.

OTEPPE January/21. Dull and getting colder.

Rumored that 1st Canadian Division will march through LIÈGE on 4th or 5th February at the invitation of townspeople.

OTEPPE January/22. Dull weather.

Great shortage of fuel is being experienced in this area which is felt considerably at present due to coldness of weather.

OTEPPE January/23. Cool weather.

Many rumors are travelling about regarding demobilization. No order of demobilization is yet received. Belgian newspapers contain notice of sale of 25,000 Canadian horses between 23/30 January at LIÈGE.

OTEPPE January/24. Dull.

Warning order sent to brigades and DAC regarding LIÈGE march. Selected detachments will represent Divisional Artillery.

OTEPPE January/25. Dull.

Conference of Brigades and DAC Commanders to decide on what representation will take part in LIÈGE function. The following is decided on and will be submitted to GOC Division at Conference tomorrow morning: HQs 1st CDA; HQs 1st Brigade CFA; Composite battery from 1st, 3rd and 4th Batteries; 4 gun battery from 2nd Howitzer Battery. HQs 2nd Brigade CFA; Composite battery from 5th, 6th and 7th Batteries; 4 gun battery from 48th Howitzer Battery; HQs CDAC and selected details from each section.

OTEPPE January/26. Dull and milder.

Preparations are being made for LIÈGE march. All batteries are very eager to make a good showing.

OTEPPE January/27. Mild weather.

CRA [and] Brigade and Battery Commanders attend lecture on training by Brigadier General GUGGISBERG at FUMAL. Everyone appeared to go to this lecture in a very hostile mood caused by the fact that now after the war we are being trained in the attack. The greatest satisfaction however was felt at the close of the lecture and demonstration at being present as it was exceptionally interesting and instructive.

1st Canadian Divisional Artillery Headquarters Staff, January 1919. Commander: Brigadier General H. C. Thacker CMG DSO; Brigade Major: Major A. H. Bick DSO (seated on General Thacker's right); Staff Captain: Lieutenant I. M. Macdonald; Staff Captain: Captain R. O. G. Bennett MC; RO: Lieutenant D. Pepler. (*Library and Archive of Canada*)

OTEPPE January/28. Cold.

CRA travels to MOHA to view specimen subsection of 5th Battery CFA turned out as standard for the LIÈGE march. It is ordered to be turned out tomorrow morning at 10.30 hours and all Brigade, Battery and section Commanders proceeding to LIÈGE will be present.

OTEPPE January/29. Cold.

Conference held at MOHA during morning to arrange final details for turnout of the artillery for LIÈGE march.

Staff Captain proceeds to area between HUY and LIÈGE to arrange billets.

OTEPPE January/30. Very cold with snow.

Rationing of LIÈGE parties is causing some trouble. This however ought to be straightened out by 1st February when units begin the march.

Staff Captain "A" is incapacitated for a time owing to fall on icy roads while riding.

OTEPPE January/31. Cold with more snow.

Billeting parties from Brigades and DAC are despatched to CHOKIER – FLEMALLE HAUTE area where they are met by Brigade Major. Billeting in CHOKIER is not good owing to presence of RFA details.

Great difficulty is being experienced in procuring frost nails for the units making LIÈGE march.

Diaries for February 1919

OTEPPE February/1. Cold. Roads in very bad condition for marching owing to ice.

Detachments from brigades and DAC move off from billets about 07.30 hours and arrive in CHOKIER – FLEMALLE HAUTE staging area about 16.00 hours. March is completed without incident.

Billeting is arranged in LIÈGE in vicinity of STATION DE LONGDOZ south of River MEUSE.

OTEPPE February/2. Cold with more snow.

Detachments move from Staging Area to LIÈGE arriving at destinations quite early. Billets are quite good although considerable difficulty was experienced by billeting officers in finding them.

OTEPPE February/3. Cold.

CRA Travels to LIÈGE to traverse route of ceremonial march with brigade and DAC Commanders. Assembly positions are also indicated.

OTEPPE February/4. Cold weather until afternoon when snow begins falling.

The Parade of the Canadians at Liège is carried out with a great sense of occasion. The Canadians are formally welcomed as the liberators of the city after the years of enemy occupation. It is also the final occasion where horses and much equipment are required. It marks an end to the work of the Canadian Expeditionary Force after over four years of active service.

All units are assembled by 10.15 hours along Rue de LEOPOLD and along QUAI's of River MEUSE.

March commences about 10.40 hours and is carried out in good style.

Cheering LIÈGOIS line the streets along the whole parade.

LIÈGE papers mentioned in their accounts particularly the artillery and the Scottish Troops.

After the review a reception is held by the Burgomaster at the Hotel de Ville followed by a luncheon to which all General officers of the Division and selected senior officers are invited.

In the evening dances for officers and for men are given by the town.

OTEPPE February/5. Cold weather.

Units march from LIÈGE to CHOKIER – FLEMALLE HAUTE Staging area.

Late in evening word is received from Divisional HQs that General Rawlinson, 4th Army Commander, will probably inspect the Division at HUY on the 7th. If this materializes Units will billet tomorrow night in AMSIN Area. Warning is despatched to units by DRLS.

OTEPPE February/6. Cold weather with more snow.

Inspection at HUY is postponed for the present.

Units march to their own billets in HUY area.

CRA attends conferences on demobilization at RA Canadian Corps at NODOIGNE.

OTEPPE February/7. [Brigadier H. C. THACKER writes diary from now on] Very cold.

Intimation is received that the Divisional Artillery will commence entraining for HAVRE about the 16th inst. All horses and equipment to be handed in before entraining.

OTEPPE February/8. Fine and very cold.

Preliminary arrangements made for handing in stores and ordinance at HUY.

OTEPPE February/9. Fine and very cold.

Conference of Battery Commanders at which Staff Captain explains arrangements for handing in stores which is to commence on 10th.

OTEPPE February/10. Fine and very cold.

1st Brigade CFA turned in guns, ammunition and vehicles. Major A H Bick DSO Brigade Major 1st CDA left for England to take a university course during period of demobilization.

OTEPPE February/11. Fine and cold.

2nd Brigade CFA turned in guns, ammunition and vehicles.

OTEPPE February/12. Fine, slightly milder.

1st Canadian Division Ammunition Column turned in vehicles and ammunition. 1st Brigade CFA turned in harness.

OTEPPE February/13. Fine, frosty.

2nd Brigade CFA turned in harness.

Colonel Arthur Hardie Bick DSO, Allied Control Comission, Germany, 1946.

OTEPPE February/14. Cloudy, thaw.

1st CDAC turned in harness to store. Intimation received that the Divisional Artillery would be the last of the 1st Canadian Division troops to leave for England in accordance with request from authorities BRAMSHOTT.

OTEPPE February/15. Dull and mild.

Units complete the return of small stores to Ordnance and have now nothing left except what is necessary for cookery and shoeing and care of horses. Word is received that owing to transport difficulties in England no troops of 1st Canadian Division will be despatched until 1st March.

There are no further entries in the war diaries of the 1st Canadian Divisional Artillery. Troops returned home in stages via camps in England, but many remained in camps in England for several months. Some of the more fortunate still had relations in Great Britain whom they could get leave to visit. Individuals were given the choice of places in Canada where they wish to be demobilised, but there is some frustration and boredom leading to unrest among those kept waiting in England. These delays were regrettable but unavoidable due to the large numbers of men wishing to return to North America and the shortage of suitable ships.

Major A. H. Bick remained in England where he practised as a civil engineer until 1938, when he joined the British Ministry of Works and engaged in airfield construction in Malta, England and Scotland throughout the Second World War. He had expressed a wish to return to military service at the beginning of the war, but was retained by the Ministry of Works to continue his work on airfields, which was deemed to be a more important contribution to the war effort. Major Bick died in an air accident at London Airport when he was returning from Brussels in February 1948.

Detail from picture on p. 80. (*Courtesy of the RCA Museum*)

Glossary

ADV: Assistant Director of Veterinary Services.

AFA: Australian Field Artillery.

Air Lines: Telephone cables mounted above ground on poles. Not very practical when positions changed frequently as they did in the mobile warfare of 1918. Later tended to be replaced by wireless communication which was vulnerable to enemy interception.

Air Recuperator: This was introduced to replace oil recuperators used to absorb the recoil on firing and return the gun to its original position, minimising the shock of these movements which would otherwise disturb the position of the gun.

Anti-Tank Guns: As the enemy increasingly employed tanks to support their infantry attacks, field guns were employed in this role. They were deployed in forward positions, often risking being overrun, in their attempts to disrupt enemy tank attacks.

ARP: Ammunition Refilling Point.

Artillery Headquarters locations: This is given as the first item on each day's diary entry. When the war was relatively static, the HQ would be established in a convenient building or, later in 1918, dugouts located not far from the front.

BC: Battery Commander.

Bde/Brigade: Units of infantry or tanks.

Btn/Battn/Battalion: Units making up brigades of infantry or tanks.

Bty/Battery: Units making up artillery brigades, battery which is normally composed of six guns of field artillery. This was increased from four guns in 1917.

Camouflage creeping barrage: Term used to describe a particular method of intimidating or disrupting enemy activity.

Canadian Artillery: 18-pdr field guns were widely used by both British and Canadian field artillery units. Units of Heavy Artillery were commanded at Corps level. There was good coordination of all artillery units in the Canadian Corps by the Counter Battery Staff Office (CBSO) when necessary. Ammunitions included high explosive, shrapnel and gas shells.

Canadian Corps organisation: From the beginning of 1917 the Canadian Corps was made up of four divisions. In 1918 these divisions were strengthened rather than using scarce resources for two further divisions. However, a fifth Divisional Artillery group (5th CDA coordinated by the CBSO) was formed to make the Canadian Corps artillery even stronger. Each Canadian division had its own Divisional Engineering Group and its infantry brigades were maintained at four battalions later on in 1918; other British infantry Brigades were reduced to three Battalions.

CBSO: Counter Battery Staff Office. This was formed, under Lieutenant Colonel Andrew McNaughton, as a part of the Canadian heavy artillery staff group at Corps level, to coordinate the management of heavy artillery to better destroy enemy gun positions. The CBSO coordinated intelligence information from sound ranging, flash spotting and air and ground observation reports. Later on, and especially during 1918, it was extended to include coordination of responses to SOS calls by all available field artillery units as well. This enabled the Canadian Corps to inflict great damage on enemy troops concentrating prior to assaults.

CCRC: Canadian Corps Reinforcement Camp.

CDA: Canadian Divisional Artillery.

CDAC: Canadian Divisional Ammunition Column. Logistical units providing transport, usually horse-drawn even in later stages of the war, for the movement of ammunition.

CDTMG: Canadian Divisional Trench Mortar Group.

CFA: Canadian Field Artillery of a divisional artillery force.

C I Bde: Canadian Infantry Brigade.

CRA: Commander Royal Artillery. This title was used for the divisional artillery commanders of both British and Commonwealth units.

Creeping Barrage: An artillery function that plans to lay down a line of shell fire just in front of advancing infantry. Typically a creeping barrage would be timed to lift 100 yards every three minutes, the speed of infantry moving on foot. Canadian infantry was trained, before the Battle of Vimy Ridge in 1917, to walk at this speed. General Currie said that he expected his infantry to keep up this rate of advance so that, unlike at the Battle of the Somme, the enemy would have no time to recover before the infantry was upon them.

CW Wireless: Continuous wave wireless communication.

DADV: Deputy Assistant Director of Veterinary Services.

DMGO: Divisional Machine Gun Officer.

DRL: Despatch Rider Liaison Service.

Drum Fire: Term used to describe a particular method of intimidating or disrupting enemy activity.

Field Artillery: Artillery employed mainly in direct support of the infantry. However, Field Artillery from individual Divisions could also be called upon by the CBSO to act in concert with heavy batteries to strike enemy artillery or infantry concentrations preparing to raid or assault.

Flash Spotting: The flash when a gun was fired could be seen by forward Observation Posts on the ground and aircraft and observation balloons in the air.

"G": General Staff, the staff branch responsible for operations and intelligence.

Gas Projection: Methods employed by the Allies were mainly in gas-filled shells fired by field artillery. Projection from gas cylinders depended on winds being light and in the right direction. Dangerous if wind was unreliable.

German guns: Terms used in the diaries to describe enemy guns are confusing because imperial and metric measurements are both used randomly:

> 5.9 (15 cm) Howitzer (also Field Gun)
> 8 cm Anti-Aircraft Gun
> 10.5 cm Howitzer
> 4.2 (10.5 cm) Howitzer
> 7.7 cm Field Gun
> 5.9 (15 cm) Field Gun (also Howitzer)

GOCRA: Canadian Corps General Officer Commanding Royal Artillery.

Gotha: Enemy aircraft frequently used during bombing missions. Later in the war, Allied air superiority during daytime operations ensured that they were only able to operate effectively after dark.

GSO1: General Staff Officer Grade 1.

Gunner: The rank equivalent of a Private soldier in the infantry, but loosely used to describe all ranks in the artillery.

HAG: Heavy artillery group. Refers to heavy and long-range artillery units.

Hill 70: A small hill overlooking the town of Lens. It was taken by the Canadians shortly after Vimy Ridge in spite of determined enemy resistance.

Hindenburg Line: A series deep defensive positions constructed by the enemy following advances made into France and Belgium in 1914–15.

HTM: Heavy trench mortars (usually 6-inch Newtons) but sometimes 9.45-inch referred to later in the 1918 campaign.

HV: High Velocity.

Illuminated Gun Sights: Special sights used to facilitate night firing.

IOM: Scrap.

Joyride shoot: Term used to describe a particular method of intimidating or disrupting enemy activity.

Lewis Gun: Machine gun firing .303 ammunition employed for battlefield and anti-aircraft roles (lighter and more portable than the Vickers machine gun).

Light Stokes: Smaller calibre trench mortars.

MGs: Machine guns. These were sometimes formed to operate as mobile units in lightly armoured vehicles to keep up with rapidly advancing infantry in 1918. General Currie regarded machine guns as light artillery in close support of infantry units.

Monkey Puzzle Barrage: Term used to describe a particular method of intimidating or disrupting enemy activity.

Newtons 6-inch: Larger calibre trench mortars used in close infantry support. Portability became problematic under mobile warfare conditions.

Observation Balloons: Airborne observation posts with hydrogen-filled balloons, raised on cables to enable observation of activities behind enemy lines. Very vulnerable to ground fire and to enemy aircraft. Personnel suspended in baskets beneath the balloon had recourse to primitive parachutes in emergency; that they were very reluctant to use except in dire emergency.

OP: Observation post set up to observe enemy positions and the shell fall of artillery. Usually in exposed locations overlooking the front line.

ORs: Other ranks, i.e. personnel other than officers.

Pigeon Service: A much-used method of communication under arduous conditions.

RFA: Royal Field Artillery.

Rnds: Rounds of ammunition.

SBR: Small Box Respirator carried by all personnel later in 1918 as a defensive measure against gas attack or when called on to operate where gas had recently been used in mobile warfare.

SOS Lines: Artillery shoots are often requested by infantry commanders to disrupt enemy building up to mount a raid or assault on their positions. The

SOS line is the line beyond which it is required to bring down fire, avoiding friendly positions. The SOS was usually sited on the most critical area and guns were laid on SOS tasks when not employed on other targets.

Sound Ranging: A relatively new technique using oscillographs to detect sound pressure waves using several microphones and comparing the times when sound is received at each one. This provided much more information about each gun's position and calibre than had been available hitherto. The German equivalents were not as highly developed.

Struck off (strength): A term used to indicate that an officer had left the established strength of a unit perhaps before being formally taken on by another unit. It is not, despite the words used, a derogatory term.

Switch: A term used to describe a strong point, or fortress, in a defensive system, designed to defend against a successful breakthrough on either side.

T.M: Trench Mortar.

Very Lights: Hand-held, pistol-operated, rocket-propelled coloured flares used in signalling, particularly useful in an emergency situation.

Wagon Lines: The name given to the location where the teams and ammunition wagons are kept while the guns are in action.

Carriage Field QF 18-pdr Mk I to Mk II. (*Courtesy of the RCA Museum*)

Bibliography

Belgian Federal Information Service, *The Monarchy in Belgium*. Belgian Government: Federal Information Service, 1999.

Cammearts, Emile, *King Albert I, Defender of the Right*. Nicolson and Watson, 1935.

Canadian National Archive: Microfilm; RG9 Militia and Defence. Series III-D-3, Volume 4958, Reel T-10775, Files 507–8.

Clarke, Dale, *British Artillery 1914–1919*. Oxford Osprey, 2004.

Cook, Tim, *Shock Troops*. Penguin Group (Canada), 2008.

Currie, Lieutenant General A. W., *Canadian Corps Operations in the year 1918*. Interim Report, Department of Militia and Defence, Ottawa, 1920.

Galet, Emile Joseph, *King Albert I in the Great War*. Putnam, 1931.

Howard, Sir Michael, *The First World War*. OUP, 2002.

Jackson, Lieutenant Colonel H. M., *The Royal Regiment of Artillery, Ottawa 1855–1952*. Canada (s.n.), 1952.

Jäger, Lieutenant Colonel Herbert, *German Artillery of World War One*. Crowood Press, 2001.

Liddell Hart, B. H., *History of the First World War*. Cassell, 1970.

Nicholson, Colonel G. W. L., *The Gunners of Canada – The History of the Royal Regiment of Canadian Artillery, Vol. 1, 1534–1919*. McClelland and Stewart, 1967.

Nicholson, Colonel G. W. L., *Canadian Expeditionary Force 1914–1919*. The Queen's Printer, Ottawa, 1962.

MacDonald Lieutenant J. A. (ed), *Gun Fire*. The Greenway Press, Toronto.

Schreiber, Shane B., *Shock Army of the British Empire*. Vanwell, 1997.

Secretaries to King Albert, *Diaries of engagements and travels 1918*. Unpublished handwritten diaries held in the Royal Archive, Brussels.

Swettenham J., *McNaughton, Vol. 1*. Ryerson Press, Toronto, 1968.

Thielemans, Marie-Rose, *Albert I, Carnets et Correspondence de Guerre 1914–1918*. Louvain-la-Neuve, Duculot, 1991.

Urquhart, H. M., *Arthur Currie: The Biography of a Great Canadian*. Dent, 1950.

Van der Kloot, Dr W., 'Lawrence Bragg's Role in the Development of Sound Ranging in World War 1', *Rec. R. Soc.* (2005) 59, 273–84.

Woolwich Artillery Museum, *Royal Regiment of Artillery Commemoration Book 1914–1918*. Royal Artillery Institution, London.

Index